CUBA

0   50   100 Kilometers

0   50   100 Miles

THE BAHAMAS

Atlantic Ocean

edios

Caibarién

Placetas

Sancti Spíritus

SANCTI SPÍRITUS

Morón

CIEGO DE AVILA

Ciego de Avila

Florida

Nuevitas

Camagüey

CAMAGÜEY

Puerto Padre

LAS TUNAS

Las Tunas

Banes

Holguín

Antilla

Santa Cruz del Sur

Amancio

HOLGUÍN

Mayarí

Moa

Baracoa

Manzanillo

Bayamo

SANTIAGO DE CUBA

GUANTÁNAMO

Palma Soriana

Guantánamo

GRANMA

Cobre

Santiago de Cuba

Pilón

HAITI

JAMAICA

CUBA

400 YEARS OF ARCHITECTURAL HERITAGE

CUBA

400 YEARS OF ARCHITECTURAL HERITAGE

RACHEL CARLEY

PHOTOGRAPHY BY ANDREA BRIZZI

WHITNEY LIBRARY OF DESIGN

AN IMPRINT OF WATSON-GUPTILL PUBLICATIONS

For all Cubans everywhere.

ACKNOWLEDGMENTS

Very special thanks to Lohania Aruca Alonso and Mario Coyula Cowley in Havana. This book would not have been possible without their time, support, and expertise. We are also indebted to Tony Mederos Alfonso, Patricia Rodríguez Aloña, Roberto López Bastida, Neri Battaglini, René Caparrós, Miguel Coyula, Mercedes Sanchez Cruz, Irán Milán Cuétara, Stephanie Davies, Jeffrey DeLaurentis, Javier DeLeon, Eduardo González Delgado, Magdalena Mustelier Dominguez, Roberto Vittloch Fernández, Ziva Freiman, Roberto López García, Francisco Joel Pérez González, Juan Luis Hernandez, Nelson Melero Lazo, Sandra Levinson, Marsha Melnick, Francisco Luna Marrero, Rafael Rojas Hurtado de Mendoza, Susan Meyer, Cecilia Olin, Victor Echengosía Peña, Micaela Porta, William Gattorno Rangal, Felix de la Noval Ravelo, María del Rosario Guerra, Olga María Ruíz Quintana, Isabel Hechavarria Ramirez, Giselle Reynaldo Reyes, Omar López Rodríguez, Raúl Rodríguez, Raúl Ruíz, Marcella Santini, Zoila Cuadras Sola, Carlos Sotolongo, and Nancy Benitez Vásquez.

Finally, this book would not have been possible without the significant scholarship on Cuban architecture and history by Jean-François LeJeune, Llilian Llanes, Louis A. Pérez, Eduardo Luis Rodríguez, Roberto Segre, Eduardo Teijera-Davis, Hugh Thomas, and Joaquín Weiss y Sanchez.

FROM THE PHOTOGRAPHER

I wish my contribution to this effort to be my declaration of love for the people and the island of Cuba. I had already planted many trees and have a son, so, according to Martí's prescription, all I was missing was a book. When I first conceived the idea of producing a book on Cuban architecture, I could not have imagined how the island would change me.

Islands, and more so large ones, breed peculiarity—of the cultural as well as natural forms; they absorb influences and make them their own. Cuba is an island in more ways than one, and all the years of isolation from the country to which it had been so close, if nothing else, have made it more "exotic." An exoticism not of space but of time, because in Cuba nothing gets thrown out: not old cars, not old songs, and certainly not the architecture.

To paraphrase Balzac, every great architecture conceals a great injustice. Cuba has had its share of both. I hope my photographs do justice to their subject, a country that is such an emotional tangle of metaphors as to leave no one indifferent.

—Andrea Brizzi

© 1997 by Rachel Carley and Andrea Brizzi
Published in 1997 by Whitney Library of Design, an imprint of Watson-Guptill Publications, a division of BPI Communications, Inc., 1515 Broadway, New York, NY 10036.

Library of Congress Cataloging-in-Publication Data
Carley, Rachel.
    Cuba: 400 Years of architectural heritage / Rachel Carley; photography by Andrea Brizzi.
    p. cm.
    Includes bibliographical references and index.
    ISBN 0-8230-1129-1
    1. Architecture—Cuba. I. Title.
    NA803.C27 1997   97-9188
    720'.97291—dc21   CIP

Manufactured in Italy

First printing, 1997

1 2 3 4 5 6 7 8 9/02 01 00 99 98 97

Page 1: *Church of San Juan Bautista* in Matanzas.

Pp. 2–3: *Church of San Francisco* in Trinidad.

Photographs on page 107, bottom, and page 117 by Rachel Carley.

Editor: Micaela Porta
Designer: Jay Anning / Thumbprint
Production Manager: Ellen Greene

CONTENTS

INTRODUCTION

By air, the trip from Miami to Havana takes less than an hour, but anyone who has made the ninety-mile journey across the Florida Straits knows that it is a deceptive measure of the real distance between Cuba and the rest of the world. Nearly four decades after the 1959 revolution that put Fidel Castro in power, this island republic of eleven million remains a country in painful transition, where socialist ideology has failed to reconcile itself with the reality of deprivation. Despite significant gains in providing access to education and health care, the recent loss of Soviet subsidies and the cumulative effects of the U.S. trade embargo continue to throttle an economy already plagued by internal mismanagement. Entire towns seem to have sidestepped the currents of time, while the effects of neglect are everywhere apparent: Paint peels, walls sag, and storefronts stand eerily empty.

At once remarkably advanced and strangely backward, Cuba has always traced a history of striking contradictions. In the centuries since Christopher Columbus discovered the largest of the Antilles in 1492, it has been coveted, colonized, exploited, maligned for its decadence, and exalted for its mystery and beauty. Here is an island that claimed the first railroad in the Spanish-speaking world, yet had no central highway until 1931; that named its colonial sugar plantations after saints but supported them with slaves; that kept a brutal dictator in power, but denied him membership to an exclusive Havana club because he was a mulatto.

Traveling around Cuba today, it is hard to shake the sense that current problems have frozen the country in a strange kind of limbo where it remains stubbornly suspended between past memory and future hope. Yet while Cubans encounter incomprehensible scarcities in every course of daily life, they are the most generous and resourceful people in the world. Soap and gasoline may be difficult to come by, but Cubans never stint on hospitality. Rum flows, music plays, ideas are shared, and somehow you eventually get to where you need to go—with six or seven extra cousins, friends, and assistants along

for the ride. In the end, it is impossible to remain unemotional about this odd, passionate, lovely, sad country. Once you've seen the moon rise over *El Morro* or heard the melancholic strains of a Cuban bolero floating from a *Casa de Trova,* you know the island has worked its way irrevocably under your skin. It knows it, too.

Scarcity, of course, has also proven a great preserver, and the lack of development has left a storehouse of remarkable structures and entire cities that not only span four centuries of Cuban history, but also remain virtually untouched by contemporary intrusions and modern-day urban sprawl. Unfortunately, this exceptional asset is increasingly in peril. Although a strong and comprehensive state preservation program designed to protect individual monuments, whole towns, and natural sites was instituted in the 1970s, the Cuban government recently launched an aggressive development plan that has made tourism the island's fastest-growing earner of hard currency. As a direct result of the push for foreign visitors, which generated gross revenues of $1.25 billion in 1996, restoration activity has stepped up in historic centers, where an increasing number of colonial buildings are being renovated for income-producing restaurants and souvenir shops. At the same time, luxury resorts are starting to consume Cuban beaches at a staggering rate. Many of the restoration and new construction projects are joint ventures between the Cuban state and foreign firms that Fidel Castro has actively courted since the 1989 breakup of the Eastern bloc drastically cut into Cuban trade.

In its rush to develop tourism, the Cuban state is often at odds with its own preservation efforts. In large part, the complex legal setup, which defines "national patrimony" as part of the constitution, was a reactive measure against the rampant and often corrupt real estate speculation of the 1950s, when several Havana landmarks were sacrificed to development projects backed by the Fulgencio Batista regime that Castro overthrew.

Preservation legislation has made a significant contribution to protecting Cuba's assets,

with new sites declared national monuments every year. But signing the notion of Cuban patrimony into national law also reflects an important political motivation.

Implicit in such legislation is the effort to establish a collective, or national, identity that is fundamental to Marxist-Leninist ideology and the populist support of a centralized government. In Cuba, even *history* is politicized, and from the Cuban viewpoint, it follows that this history is theirs to save—or sell—as Cubans see fit.

Caught between the State preservation program and the drive for commercial and related tourist development are many dedicated and enlightened historians, urban planners, architects, and conservationists who are working to protect the island's remarkable built environment. Both Old Havana and the colonial city of Trinidad, together with its nearby Valle de los Ingenios, have been declared World Heritage Sites by UNESCO in recognition of their historic, archi-

tectural, and archeological value. However, almost no funds have been forthcoming as a result. And even if money and materials were available, no amount could save an entire country of structures that have gone largely unmaintained for forty years. The rubble-filled lots in every city are testimony to the fact that buildings collapse daily, sometimes when materials are pirated for other projects. In a year or two, it will make more sense to demolish crumbling neighborhoods rather than try to preserve what is there.

This book, then, is not only a celebration of an extraordinary timeline of history, but a documentation of what is here now but will likely disappear soon. We hope to call attention to this unparalleled resource and share it in the belief that, of all Cuba's many attributes, none speaks more eloquently of the island's evolution and revolution than its architecture.

RACHEL CARLEY
Washington, Connecticut
September, 1997

Fronted by a wide veranda, a fisherman's house in Cayo Granma typifies the simple wood-frame houses found in Cuba's coastal settlements.

CUBAN ROOTS

Like the country itself, Cuban architecture defies easy categorization. Although there are certain bonds with other Caribbean and Latin American countries, architecture here still has a distinct but difficult-to-define *Cuban* spirit. One primary reason is that Cuba's history followed its own peculiar route, shaped by an extended period of colonization—beginning with the first Spanish settlement in 1512—and the concomitant development of an island culture that was geographically self-contained, dependent for centuries on the outside world, then, finally, largely cut off from it.

In particular, Cuba differed from its sister colonies in the island's extraordinarily long tenure under the shadow of the Spanish monarchy. Although the once-vast imperial empire in Latin America had all but disintegrated by 1825, Cuba's reluctance to jeopardize her stupendously lucrative slave economy checked the colony's move for independence long after every other Spanish Caribbean possession but Puerto Rico had broken free. When the Spanish-American War culminated in a final breach with Spain in 1898, it marked the end of a colonial period that had lasted the better part of four hundred years.

This protracted relationship had as much effect on the physical fabric of Cuba as it did on its social and economic development. Far ahead of England or France, Spain consistently approached colonization of the New World from the standpoint of urban planning. Establishing a logical, well-designed, well-defended city was a way to assert control and command respect. Imperial interests in Cuba resulted in a long series of strong governors who commissioned new city plans and imposing civic buildings as imprints of power and monuments to their own egos, while shaping a long-lasting military character for the island.

As elsewhere in Latin America, the first and most important architects in Cuba were European military engineers, part of a group of accomplished professionals charged with developing a comprehensive fortification system for the Caribbean. Havana's early infrastructure included not only a vast string of coastal forts, but also the 1592 *Zanja Real* aqueduct, among the earliest European-built water-supply systems in the Americas, and the extensive fortified walls surrounding Havana, which were begun in 1665.

Considered the most significant architectural achievements of the period in the Caribbean, these engineering feats also represented the first form of economic development in Cuba. They demanded an established and organized labor force. This consisted primarily of prisoners and slaves (rented at a day rate from their owners), who learned bricklaying, stone cutting, and other building skills from a corps of trained artisans. A related hierarchy of labor (which included mulattos and blacks as well as whites) lasted for centuries, and traces of it remain even today.

As direct envoys of the monarchy, military engineers were accorded considerable prestige, and also oversaw important government and church projects. Because they ranked so high among building professionals, they played a strong role in Cuban architecture well into the 19th century. By an 1846 Spanish decree, the right to design *ensanches,* or city expansions, for example, went not to architects, but exclusively to engineers. The *Escuela de Ingenieros* in Madrid assured graduates government positions and assigned them jobs in the American colonies. Engineers oversaw urban renewal programs, framed building codes, directed public works programs, and continued to design and review important projects throughout much of the republican period.

Military engineers Silvestre Abarca and Pedro de Medina were commissioned to build the Fortaleza de San Carlos de la Cabaña *after the British invaded Havana in 1762. Entered by monumental baroque portal, the complex contained a plaza, batteries, stables, chapel, roads, and gardens.*

CRAFTSMAN AND ARCHITECT

From the start, the artisan played a primary role in building Cuba. With the exception of the European military engineers dispatched to the Antilles and the mainland Caribbean coast, Spain directed her best architectural talent to Mexico and Peru during the early colonial period. The building of the first settlements on the island, considered a relatively unimportant backwater until the mid-18th-century sugar boom, fell to self-schooled friars among the religious missionary orders and to the immigrant peasants, who initially adopted the palm-thatch construction methods of Cuba's indigenous Arawak Indians. Bricklayers, stonecutters, and woodworkers, including the skilled *Mudéjar,* or Spanish-Moorish, craftsmen were also among the very early

Rosehead nails hand-wrought from iron stud a wood-plank entrance in a style referred to as "a la española." The large carriage port incorporates two smaller doors for humans.

CUBAN ROOTS

Spanish settlers, and these so-called practical builders would help establish a deeply rooted emphasis on manual labor and craft.

In particular, that emphasis depended on the persistence of a long-standing tradition of teaching building skills through hands-on experience. At the time the island was settled in the early 1500s, education in building and design was still loosely based on a medieval guild system of apprenticeship training. Although formal academic education in architecture was instituted in Europe by the mid-1700s, the first educational programs in building or architecture were not established in Cuba until a century later. Even then, the pressing need for workers to build plantations and the commercial centers supporting them put the majority of work into the hands of the practical builder who learned on the job, rather than in an academy.

Outside of the engineer—whose work was limited to major military projects and cathedrals—the highest ranking builder in early colonial Cuba was in fact a well-trained artisan known as the *maestro de obras,* or master of works. While an experienced master craftsman (often a stonecutter or mason), this professional was also capable of drawing and executing designs based on the accepted conventions of the day. He refined and oversaw projects for the military engineers, and commissioned the stone and woodcarvers and other artisans needed to complete forts, cathedrals, major churches, and the grand *palacios* of the Creole aristocracy.

Professional builders in early colonial Cuba also carried a number of other titles, including *alarife* (a term of Mudéjar origin), which loosely translates as "architect," or *maestro arquitecto* (roughly, "master architect"). The differences signified by these often-interchangeable names are not clear, but all titles recognized a significant level of responsibility and expertise earned through apprenticeship with a master.

Under the 18th-century Bourbon monarchy, the contemporary concept of designer (versus builder-artisan) began to emerge in Spain, but was slow to take hold in Cuba, partly because the monarchy remained relatively uninterested in the architectural development of its remote island colony. Following a deep-rooted prejudice against manual occupations, traditionally forbidden to the Spanish nobility, the Bourbons moved to reorganize the building professions into a de-

liberate hierarchy and establish the French practice of state-controlled academies. This was intended to secure a set standard of taste by endowing the architect with particular prestige and power while curtailing the role of master builder, who was of lower social standing.[1]

As part of the centralized arts movement, an Academy of Fine Arts was established in Madrid in 1744 and formalized in 1757, granting students the title of architect. In the absence of an equivalent institution, Cubans had to travel to Spain for accredited higher education in the field. But as an elitist career, architecture was available only to the few Creoles who could afford the trip abroad or were permitted to spend the time away from the family business. The title of *"arquitecto"* was of little consequence in 18th-century Cuba, where the old traditions held strong.

Although prejudice against manual trades also existed in Cuba, the 19th-century implementation of educational programs in architecture, planning, and building had less to do with defining the status of various design and building professions than with the practical economic and political goals of the monarchy. Reforms occurred mainly when it became clear that Spain could not build the roads, bridges, and buildings needed to support her lucrative capital investment in the sugar economy without training Cubans in related disciplines. Furthermore, it was believed that a new emphasis on technical careers would divert young, fertile minds away from intellectual pursuits like law—considered more likely to engender political ferment in a climate already leaning dangerously toward independence from Spain or possible annexation to the United States.

Intended to ensure standards for the quality of design and building, the first professional school (repeatedly renamed and reorganized) in Cuba opened at the preparatory level in the mid-1800s. The *Escuela Profesional* offered courses in mechanical drawing, surveying, construction, landscape design, and architectural history. Among the titles granted graduates was the formal *maestro de obras.* But until a school of architecture and engineering was created in 1900 at the University of Havana, it was still necessary to seek accreditation as a titled architect outside of Cuba, where the profession of master builder remained firmly entrenched.

AN EVOLUTION OF STYLE

Cuba can claim only a handful of buildings that can be called "high style" by any conventional measure. Indeed, its architecture is significant not so much for its great individual moments, but as a collective timeline of buildings in which craft, material, detail, and a peculiarly Cuban sense of color and ornament mean everything. One of the reasons it is so easy to respond to Cuban architecture is that it conveys an immediate sense of the hand at work, along with unabashed pleasure in texture and detail, and a gift for completely unselfconscious eccentricity.

As is true of any vernacular architecture, Cuban building is the product of a long process of adaptation, drawing on an amalgam of cultural traditions, climatic conditions, fashion, taste, and preference for materials. Although some volcanic paving stone (*losa isleña*) was imported from the Canary Islands, the majority of early building was done with native materials, including an excellent hard stone quarried in the area of San Miguel and in Havana. Indigenous woods—especially the extremely hard varieties of *ácana, jiquí,* and *quiebrahacha,* as well as ebony and cedar—were used widely on the island for construction and shipbuilding and also were valued for export.

In particular, early colonial Cuban architecture reflects the influence of the *Mudéjares* (later called *Moriscos*), who were among the few Arab minorities remaining in Spain under Christian rule after the 15th-century reconquest of the Moors. With medieval Arabic roots, the Mudéjar tradition was inherently decorative, and—significantly for Cuba—represented a great heritage of artistry and craftsmanship. The work of Mudéjar craftsmen was so highly regarded that after the reconquest these skilled bricklayers, woodcarvers, and plasterworkers often served as vassals to the Spanish aristocracy; many also became attached to monasteries, as bequeathing their services to the Church was regarded as a great act of devotion.

In the 17th and early 18th centuries, the Mudéjar effect on Cuban architecture was readily apparent in the use of decorative clay tile, deep wooden eaves, and latticework windows and balconies found in the southern Spanish vernacular. It is especially notable in the intricately pieced ceilings known as *alfarjes*—layered with geometric prism and star patterns—that still distinguish so many 18th-century Cuban houses and churches today. The preference for enclosed, subdivided spaces and the inner patio, found in domestic and religious architecture, is also a Moorish legacy.

Tinted glass vitrales *designed to filter the bright Caribbean sun also answered the Cuban taste for color and pattern. Such windows were probably introduced in the late 1700s.*

Much has also been made of the Spanish baroque in colonial architecture, but in Cuba the baroque style was almost always vernacular in interpretation. Characterized by a dynamic sense of movement and rich embellishment, the baroque had its most intense expression in Roman Catholic countries, sweeping into Spain in the early 1600s. Compelling imagery and an inherent sense of ceremony made a natural psychological link with the Church's efforts to reestablish authority during the late stages of the Counter-Reformation, and coincided well with Spain's zealous missionary activity in Latin America.

The greatest impact of the baroque in Cuba can, in fact, be seen in the island's church architecture. But even the dynamically curved facade of the 1777 Havana Cathedral, considered the most mature example of Cuban baroque, is sedate in comparison to the exuberantly treated Mexico Cathedral in Mexico City or *La Compañia* in Cuzco, Peru. The baroque aesthetic did, however, flourish in Cuba's church interiors. Eighteenth-century churches throughout the island still contain fantastic gilded altars and *retablos,* or altar-pieces. These are profusely worked in fruit and floral motifs in the frenzied style of the Churrigueras, a family of influential architects and sculptors working in Castile in the late 17th and early 18th centuries.

Used from the 16th century well into the 20th, ceramic tiles (right) recall a Mudéjar craft tradition that flourished in southern Spain during the Middle Ages. The use of decorative painted bands known as cenefas *(above), is believed to date to the 1600s. The practice began to flourish while Spain was under Bourbon rule in the late 1700s, when designs reflected European influences.*

The Cuban alfarje *incorporates inclining and horizontal beams in a roofing method called* par y nudillo. *The Moorish custom of piecing wood in intricate designs derives from Arabia, where longer lengths of lumber were scarce. Black detailing was done with a mixture of rabbit glue, water, and soot. Star patterns signified the magnitude of the universe.*

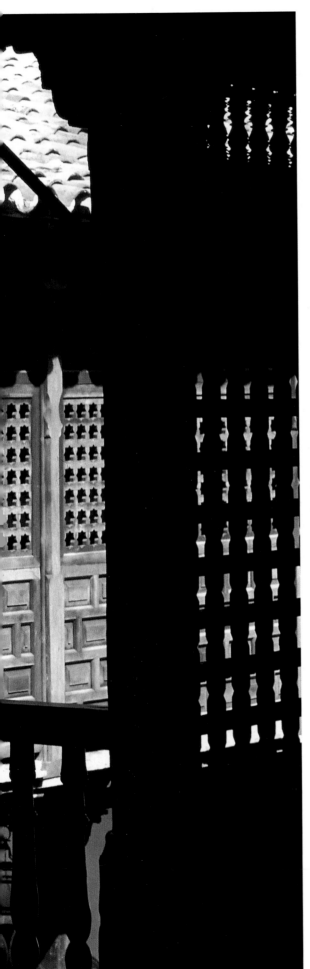

Celosias, *intricate latticework window screens made of cedar (left), and* rejas *with turned spindles (above) served as ventilating window screens. Both elements derive from Moorish architecture.*

The block-long convent and corner church of Nuestra Señora de Belén *in Havana was begun in 1712 and remodeled in the 19th and early 20th centuries.*

CUBA: 400 YEARS OF ARCHITECTURAL HERITAGE

The opposing planes of the facade of the 1777 Havana Cathedral (below) reflect one of the most mature expressions of the Spanish baroque in Cuba. The design inspired the facade of the nearby Real Colegio Seminario de San Carlos y San Ambrosio *(left), which dates to the 1700s, but was remodeled in the neo-baroque style in 1950.*

Stonework for the door of the Casa de la Obra Pía (right) was executed in Cádiz around 1686, then shipped to Cuba. The house was built for the Calvo de la Puerta family, headed by the Marquis of Obra Pía. A monumental baroque portal also dominates the facade of the 1738 Church of San Francisco de Asís (below) in the same city.

The other notable mark of the baroque was the taste for grandiose, sculptural doors, found primarily in Havana. Most were virtual copies of the portals embellishing the ancestral palaces of Jerez and other bay-area towns of Cádiz on the southern coast of Andalusia. The somewhat awkward appearance of the stone carvings is partly due to the fact that many of the most highly trained artisans were sent to Mexico and Peru, as well as to the porosity of the local Cuban coral-stone. The doors tend to appear pasted on, exemplifying how early Cuban builders evoked a "sense" of the baroque with details (a door, a lintel, an ornate *retablo*) rather than shaping a volumetric composition in which the parts (plan, facade, ornament) are related as a whole.

One of the most persuasive influences in Cuban colonial architecture was neoclassicism. Rooted in strict systems of proportion, geometry, and spatial function, the sedate neoclassical style emerged in mid-18th-century Europe as a timely reaction to the flamboyant eccentricities of the baroque. The taste for neoclassicism, fueled by recent archeological discoveries in ancient Greece and Rome, was especially fashionable in France, and arrived in Cuba just as the models of taste set by Francophile circles in Bourbon Spain were sifting into the Caribbean.

The first neoclassical architectural designs in Cuba were by Étienne-Sulpice Hallet, a French architect who worked on plans for the U.S. Capitol building in the 1790s and was living in Havana by 1800. Hallet's design for the *Cementerio General de la Habana* (Espada Cemetery) featured a temple-fronted chapel painted in a faux marble design and an elegant entrance portal conceived as a triumphal arch. Havana opened an academy of *bellas artes, La Academia de Pintura y Escultura de San Alejandro,* in 1818, headed by the French artist Jean Baptiste Vermay, a follower of the great French neoclassical artist Jacques-Louis David.

Neoclassicism was significant in that it affected virtually every class of Cuban building from small house to civic monument in nearly every part of the island. Classical principles were also manifested in the monumental planning and landscaped squares of new cities, most notably in Cienfuegos (1819) and in Cárdenas (1828). The rapid dissemination of classical influences throughout Cuba during the 19th century coincided with the continued growth of the

The tradition of the portal, interpreted with classical columns in the 1800s, spread to all provincial cities, including Pinar del Río (left).

Corinthian columns endow the portal of the Museo Nacional de la Música *in Havana (left) with a formality suited to an important civic building. Creating a temple-like facade, a Corinthian portico fronts a building constructed for the* Sociedad Económica de Amigos del Pais *(above), an influential civic and cultural group founded by the Creole aristocracy.*

sugar economy and related improvements in communications, both internally and with European capitals increasingly visited by the Cuban elite. It can also be credited in part to the strong cultural influence of the thousands of French coffee and sugar planters who flowed into Cuba after the 1791 slave rebellion in Haiti.

Symbolic of the high civic principles and cultural achievements of ancient civilization, neoclassicism in Cuba was initially linked to an era of intellectual growth in which an increasingly secularized climate embraced poetry, literature, theater, music, the arts, and scientific and educational development. The Cuban intellectual movement followed in the broader spirit of the 18th-century enlightenment, which questioned traditional doctrines, and emphasized empirical reasoning, universal human progress, and independent thought. It is no coincidence that Matanzas, one of the colony's most important 19th-century sugar capitals and the center of a leading intellectual circle, was known as "the Athens of Cuba."

The classical canon remained entrenched in Cuba well into the republican period. By the late 19th century, Cuban architects were deeply immersed in the Beaux Arts tradition. Students still sought architecture titles abroad since education in architecture and the building trades was as yet only offered at a preparatory level on the island. Some studied in Madrid or Paris, but many at-

Classical elements were freely mixed with details from other styles by the turn of the century, including the art nouveau (above and right) reflected in some of the column bases.

tended North American schools, most notably Rensselaer Polytechnic Institute, M.I.T., the University of Illinois, and Cornell, which were among the first North American schools to institute architecture programs.[2]

The academic tradition also persisted at the new school of architecture at the University in Havana, reorganized in 1900 by order of U.S. General Leonard Woods during North American occupation after the Spanish-American War. The five-year course of study relied on standard texts from Europe, the United States, and England, including the British publication *Elements of Architecture* by John Millington, and centered on a thorough grasp of the complete orders of the leading Renaissance architect Giacomo Barozzi da Vignola. Graduates, who had spent many hours copying plaster casts of classical statuary and building fragments from the Louvre, frequently entered competitions sponsored by Beaux-Arts societies of North American colleges.[3]

Designed in a similar spirit, both the former residence of José Gómez Mena in Havana (left) and the Royal Bank of Canada in Santiago (below) reflect the influence of North American Beaux Arts design.

North American magazines were also a powerful influence. Although Cuba's own review, *Arquitectura,* appeared in 1916 (publication stopped in 1919, then resumed in 1925), U.S. journals such as *Architectural Record, The American Architect,* and *Architectural Forum* were widely read. Moreover, Cubans held foreign architects in high esteem, and several North American firms recognized for their polished academicism, including Carrère and Hastings, McKim, Mead and White, and Walker and Gillette, left their mark on Havana.

Inherently "safe," classically inspired designs were long the choice of conservative groups, including the remnants of the disappearing aristocracy in Cuba, who saw it as a tasteful counterpoint to the flamboyant art nouveau style brought by Catalonian immigrants to Cuba in the early 1900s. History and tradition endowed classicism with acceptability; by definition, it was also a monumental mode that proved well-suited to public statements by a succession of parvenu leaders who wished to make their mark in the new republic.[4] A 1926 master plan for Havana that president Gerardo Machado (1924–33) commissioned from French landscape designer Jean-Claude Nicolas Forestier, for example, was based on Beaux-Arts principles. Components of this urban ideal, including the tiered staircase for the University of Havana, the axial, landscaped *Paseo del Prado,* one of Havana's most important thoroughfares, and the domed National Capitol, remain among the city's primary identifying elements today.

Although it dominated the public sphere, classicism played an increasingly subordinate role to the pervasive eclectic movement, which with neoclassicism was the determining stylistic factor in all Cuban cities into the 1930s. Eclecticism encompassed an idiosyncratic (sometimes bizarre) mix of several stylistic features—including classical, European revivalist, medieval,

The Trust Company of Cuba (above and right) typifies the classically inspired designs of early republican financial buildings. These replaced colonial buildings in an area of Old Havana that resembled New York's Wall Street in the early 1900s.

The classical taste had a strong influence on religious and commercial buildings throughout the island. In a 1986 reconstruction of an 18th-century Santiago church, Nuestra Señora de los Dolores, architect Manuel Quevedo retained the classical pediment added in the 1800s (left). The Italian Renaissance-inspired Lonja del Comercio (below), was designed for Havana's Plaza de San Francisco by Tomás Mur in 1909.

A classical balustrade, Ionic capitals,
and spiral columns on a house in
Ciego de Avila epitomize the use of
eclectic elements in provincial
domestic architecture.

Arabic, art nouveau, and Oriental elements—in the same design; buildings in different styles also appeared contemporaneously in the same neighborhoods. This was in part the result of rampant real estate speculation, but it also reflected the cosmopolitan airs of the new socially mobile middle class. To some extent, shuffling through styles was a trend of the times. But on a deeper level, the idea that Cuban culture could be shaped and improved by studying and interpreting the best of others had long been a current in Cuban philosophical thought. Eclectism may also reflect a kind of identity crisis in the search for roots by a newly independent country that was not entirely comfortable with its own past.

In drawing on historical periods, eclecticism was not unrelated to the Beaux-Arts movement, but there were distinct differences. Whereas the Beaux-Arts approach emphasized

"correct," bookish interpretations of the past (the essence of good taste), it certainly did not prescribe their indiscriminate combination. Moreover, in Cuban eclecticism, the sources were often so vague as to be unrecognizable.

One notable manifestation of this somewhat schizophrenic architectural taste was the relative popularity of the Spanish revival during the early decades of the 1900s. This might seem surprising given the country's recent independence. However, a powerful sector of the Spanish ruling class remained in Cuba. At the time, there was also a growing interest in the Spanish colonial architecture of Mexico.

Then, too, Spanish revival design—essentially loose interpretations of medieval and renaissance sources—was currently very fashionable for resort architecture in North America. Architects in Cuba, for example, were well aware of the influence of Bertram Goodhue's work in

Designed for a well-to-do doctor who traveled extensively, the 1909 Palacio Güasch in Pinar del Río incorporated elements inspired by architecture around the world, including Moorish arches and French Gothic spires.

CUBAN ROOTS

27

Moroccan craftsmen were brought to Cienfuegos to work on the Palacio del Valle, *a 1912 neo-Moorish mansion built by Aciclio Valle to show off his riches. He later went bankrupt.*

CUBA: 400 YEARS OF ARCHITECTURAL HERITAGE

The facade of the Hotel Sevilla *in Old Havana (left) incorporates classical columns into the neo-Moorish detailing. Built in 1908, the hotel was remodeled by the architectural firm of Arellano y Mendoza in 1923. Florid interior decor was typical of social clubs of the period, including the* Club San Carlos *in Santiago (below).*

California and Addison Mizner's imprint in Palm Beach, Florida. Indeed, North American architects, including Kenneth Murchison (Central Railway Station), McKim, Mead and White (*Hotel Nacional*), and Goodhue (*Santísima Trinidad Episcopal Cathedral;* now demolished) helped establish the style in Havana. It was also picked up by Cuban architects in projects for North American clients, such as the DuPont family, who commissioned a Spanish revival-style mansion that still dominates the beach resort of Varadero, and imported to Cuban suburbs on a more modest level in the form of the popular "California house," a simple one-story residence with such "Spanish" elements as ironwork, tiles, and a patio or courtyard.

The 1927 Spanish Revival-style Cuban Telephone Company (below and bottom) in Havana combined Churrigueresque detail with a few contemporary flourishes. The design is by Morales y Cía.

The Central Railway Station (right), designed by North American architect Kenneth Murchison in 1910, blends Spanish Revival and Italian Renaissance elements. The belltowers contain stairs, elevators, and bathrooms.

Tile insets, balconies, and baroque window frames endow an early 20th-century Vedado residence with a distinctly "Spanish" character.

In 1926, the pharmaceuticals magnate Eleuthère Irenée DuPont purchased 1265 acres of beachside property in Varadero and commissioned a Spanish revival vacation house (right and opposite, top). The design, by Evelio Govantes and Félix Cabarrocas, features Moorish balconies and details handcarved in mahogany.

CUBA: 400 YEARS OF ARCHITECTURAL HERITAGE

The Spanish Embassy in Havana (below) incorporates elements from early Cuban architecture, including the ground-floor portal and lucetas. This Spanish revival confection was designed by Francisco Ramírez Ovando in 1912.

Running concurrently with historicist architecture in Cuba was the art nouveau style, which came to the island via contemporary periodicals and a wave of immigrants from the northern Spanish regions of Catalonia, Galicia, and Asturia just after independence. Most widely associated with the Barcelona architect Antonio Gaudí y Cornet, the Spanish art nouveau was part of a broader-based intellectual *modernista* movement, itself an offshoot of the art nouveau in Paris (home to a large contingent of Catalonian intellectuals) and of the related German *Jugenstil* movement. The *modernistas* were members of a broad experimental sphere—including literature, decorative and applied arts, and architecture—that explored quality of craftsmanship, honesty of design, and organic beauty in nature in a search for new expression independent of the past. Cuban involvement with the movement reached its highest level among such literary figures as José Martí and Julián de Casal. In architecture, however, art nouveau was largely the work of immigrant builders and craftsmen

associated with the "Barcelona bourgeoisie" and was never fully accepted by the Castilian sector, which had been the political center of Spanish domination.

The somewhat later success of the art deco style in Cuba in the late 1920s and the 1930s paralleled the dawn of the transportation age and the strengthening commercial ties between Cuba and the United States. It also reflected the ongoing desire among the Cuban bourgeoisie to adopt the fashions of culturally sophisticated countries, and to keep up with the modern— and thus, fashionable—currents emerging in the United States as well as in Latin American and European capitals.

The initial phase of this early modernist mode coincided with a period of affluence and cultural activity in the years just prior to the Depression. By this time, the 1925 *Exposition Internationale des Arts Décoratifs et Industriels Modernes* in Paris had already made a strong impression on both North America and the Latin American mainland.

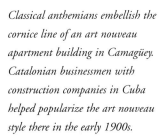

Classical anthemians embellish the cornice line of an art nouveau apartment building in Camagüey. Catalonian businessmen with construction companies in Cuba helped popularize the art nouveau style there in the early 1900s.

The art nouveau was frequently used by Cuban master builders who picked up elements such as door and tile designs from contemporary publications.

Havana's El Centro de Oro *(right), designed circa 1910 by Eugenio Dediot, incorporated ground-floor commercial space with apartments above. This layout was typical of the combined-use buildings constructed by middle-class merchants during the early 1900s. An art nouveau style window (above) retains traditional louvered shutters.*

The first use of the stylish new art deco mode in Cuba is widely considered to be in the 1927 Havana house of Francisco Argüelles, designed by José Antonio Mendigutía, and in the residence of Juan de Pedro Baró and Catalina Lasa, designed by Evelio Govantes and Félix Cabarrocas the same year. Built for a Cuban family that spent a large portion of the year in Paris, the de Pedro house had a classically inspired facade but featured fabulous art deco interiors and glasswork by the fashionable Paris designer René Lalique.

It is also significant that in this same period of the 1920s, Jean-Claude Nicolas Forestier was working on his master plan for Havana with several French planners and architects. These included Albert Laprade, who would design the deco-inspired 1931 Museum of the Colonies in Paris and Jean Labatut, who later contributed to the modernist monument to José Martí (1938–52) in Cuba's own capital.[5]

The sala and dining room of the 1927 residence of Juan de Pedro in Vedado still have their original furnishings and the glass fixtures by René Lalique, who also designed the vestibule (below). The architects were Evelio Govantes and Félix Cabarrocas; French landscape designer Jean-Claude Nicolas Forestier created the gardens.

José A. Mendigutía designed the first house in Cuba with an art deco exterior. However, the massing of the 1927 Argüelles house, located in Marianao, was typical of eclectic-style suburban villas.

In addition, the art deco influence in Cuba undoubtedly reflected Havana's proximity to Miami, where Cuban president Gerardo Machado established a consulate in 1925. A series of speculative ventures in the late 1920s and 1930s produced one of the largest concentrations of art deco hotels and small-scale apartment buildings in the world. Early Havana skyscrapers such as the 1929 headquarters for the Bacardí company also show a close kinship to New York's art deco towers, ultimate symbols of capitalist success. The relationship is clearly evident in the adoption of setbacks and of a modified base-and-shaft configuration. Both were the result of a 1916 New York zoning law that regulated the height and floor space of a building in relationship to lot size and street width.

Although it was used for residences—especially the facades of small but up-to-date houses built for Havana's petit bourgeoisie—art deco was also a popular commercial style, adapted to movie and apartment houses, office towers, department stores, and restaurants. As in Miami, the inherent modernity of the style signaled progress and the future, which was particularly important in the years immediately following the Depression. Moreover, the simple, geometric motifs were easy to assimilate and less costly to execute than the elaborate ornament lavished on eclectic houses.

By the 1920s, an intellectual modernist movement had also begun to gain momentum in Cuba, specifically among a group of young Cuban art and architecture students influenced by the contemporary Latin American vanguard movement. Early vanguard currents were primarily theoretical, but they did raise the question of how buildings might be designed with a mind to a natural, social, and *Cuban* context. On a limited basis, they also promoted the integration of Cuban sculpture and artwork with larger architectural schemes.

Embellished with colored terra-cotta, the 1930 Bacardí headquarters in Havana is the most fully realized art deco commercial building in Cuba. The design is by Esteban Rodríguez Castells, Rafael Fernández Ruenes, and José Menéndez. A bat, the Bacardí emblem, crowns the spire.

The starkly interpreted facade of the 1940s Gran Logia *in Havana represents a later phase of the art deco. The globe surmounting the roof is a typical element of the style, which flourished at a time when advances in transportation and communications started to connect Cuba to the world.*

The Casa de las Américas *in Havana employs the vertical setbacks (left) and geometrical terra-cotta motifs (below) characteristic of art-deco skyscrapers.*

The Moncada Garrison in Santiago (left) has a strong horizontal massing, punctuated with vertical ribbing, also an art deco feature. The barracks are best known as the site of a rebel attack led by Fidel Castro on July 26, 1953.

41

A modest art deco style house in the Miramar suburb of Havana dates from the 1940s, when the area started to become fashionable. Such houses typically retained a traditional layout behind their elegant facades.

The design for the modernist Banco Nacional de Cuba *in Santiago (left) took advantage of materials widely available after World War II, including plate glass and poured concrete. The streamlined design by Fernando de Zárraga and Mario Esquiroz for the 1947* Colegio de Arquitectos *in Havana (below) recalls the art deco style of the previous decade.*

A 1950s Havana residence (above) represents a sophisticated post-war rationalist design in concrete and glass; a deep roof overhang helps temper the tropical sun. Devoid of traditional references, the 1957 Clínica Antonetti *by the firm of Alvarez y Gutiérrez (right) reflected the continued Cuban interest in European rationalism.*

A private residence by Fernando Salinas and Raúl González Romero in Miramar illustrates the last phase of Cuban modernism before the 1959 revolution.

During this period of intellectual modernism, the University of Havana, a center of political and ideological debate, served as a forum for outspoken opposition to the island's cultural commercialism, pro-U.S. policy, and the lack of design integrity engendered by speculative development. Cuban theorists and educators deplored the indiscriminate plundering of historical elements to create "artistic shams."

In a 1928 issue of the journal of the architects' association, the *Colegio de Arquitectos de la Habana,* the architect Silvio Acosta declared, "The past is not a rule, it is a date." A year later, an issue of the same journal featured an article by the German architect Bruno Taut, liberally illustrated with his own minimalist apartment-house designs in Berlin. Taut outlined the basis of modernist thought, stating that "the architect should express in the plan and form of a building the social principles embodied therein."

The search to express a Cuban heritage in design and craftsmanship and growing concern for working-class interests meshed with the modernist ideal of resolving social problems through pure and honest design founded on clarity of form and function. Modernism found expression in Latin America by the 1930s, where the Corbusian influence ran deep. In 1934, Le Corbusier consulted on plans for the rationalist Ministry of Education and Health Building in Rio de Janeiro (1934), designed by a team of architects including Oscar Neimeyer, who was later credited with having a strong impact on Cuban modernists.

However, the first rationalist designs were not actually built in Cuba until the 1940s, and by this time the influence came largely from the United States rather than from Latin America. At the time, many U.S. architects were overseeing high-profile commissions in Havana, such as the U.S. embassy by the firm of Harrison and Abramovitz. (Harrison would later head the team of architects, including Oscar Neimeyer, that designed the United Nations Headquarters in New York; 1947–53). In the 1940s, the Austrian architect Richard Neutra—based in Los Angeles since the 1920s—made several visits to Havana, which were covered with interest in Cuban newspapers. The minimalist concrete-and-glass design he completed there for Alfred de Schultess in 1956 became a kind of shrine for Cuban modernists.

Exploration of contemporary European and North American currents abruptly ceased with the 1959 revolution. The highly romanticized design of the National Arts School in Havana, a utopian vision and one of the first projects created under the new government, reflects the euphoria that infused Cuba during the early days of the revolution. But the spirit of creative collaboration on this early project soon gave way to a centralized government building program based on Eastern European socialist models and geared to an ambitious program to build schools, hospitals, factories, and housing across the island.

In a climate of a Marxist-Leninist ideology directed to finding immediate solutions to social problems, artistic expressionism was meaningless in the practical context of erecting structures as cheaply and rapidly as possible. The profession of architect as it had existed before the revolution by and large disappeared. Creative team approaches continued to be explored, but only within the confines of rigid prefabrication systems that met with varied degrees of success. Architects of a few projects, such as Havana's 1964 City University (CUJAE), achieved creative spatial solutions with modular units, but most of the prefabrication projects remain devoid of architectural merit. Meanwhile, the scope of architectural education in Cuba narrowed its focus from cultural and urban matters to technical subjects in order to support the centralized program. The Cuban architect became builder, construction supervisor, and designer all in one.

One of the declared aims of the new revolutionary architecture was the elimination of "polyvalent" design and superficial symbolism that reflects class differences, in favor of a search for an architecture with a social responsibility.[6] But this brings up the question of whether buildings in want of creative or emotional purpose prove equally devoid of social worth. In 1989, and again in 1991, a group of young Cuban architects and students involved with the cultural group "Brigada Hermanos Saíz" addressed this issue with exhibitions of experimental designs supported by the architecture faculty at CUJAE and the Ministry of Construction. The first show was almost prevented from opening by the Union of Cuban Architects and Engineers. In particular, the designs explored postmodernist currents then popular in the United States while criticizing the centralized state approach to Cuban institutional architecture.[7] This period of creative exploration was both controversial and short lived. Currently, the lack of materials and finances has drastically curtailed design and construction, and the question remains open, even if debate—for the moment—does not.

State-sponsored microbrigade housing in Guantánamo shows a move away from mammoth apartment complexes to smaller one- and two-family houses in the 1990s.

CUBA: 400 YEARS OF ARCHITECTURAL HERITAGE

The forty-room Hotel Aurora *in the Vista Alegre suburb of Santiago (above) was built with the Girón system of prefabricated concrete panels. The revolutionary-period design by Sandra Alvarez includes three levels of rooms tied to a multi-level site with terraces and open spaces; services are located on the lower level. A four-story apartment building in Nueva Gerona on the Isle of Youth (left) reflects a move away from high-rise housing projects in the late 1970s and early 1980s.*

Part II

THE EARLY COLONIAL ERA

1512–1762

A bronze statue of "La Giradilla" crowning the belltower of the Castillo de la Real Fuerza *represents Doña Inés de Bobadilla, Cuba's only female governor. She replaced her husband Hernando de Soto when he left to conquer Florida in 1539.*

Colonization of the New World came at a difficult but critical point in Spanish history, just as the newly united nation struggled with the transition from medieval feudalism to capitalism. In 1492, the fall of the last Arab strongholds in Granada and Seville in the southern region of Andalusia had ended some eight centuries of Muslim rule and sealed the Christian bid for reconquest. That same year, Christopher Columbus claimed both Hispaniola and Cuba, the "Pearl of the Antilles," for Ferdinand II and Isabel I, joint rulers of Aragon (roughly eastern Spain) and Castile (roughly central-western Spain). These small islands would be the first outposts in a vast Spanish-American empire, conquered over the next fifty years and exploited as a critical resource for centuries to come.

Spain's foray into the New World was ostensibly founded on the missionary interests of the Catholic Church, but the real motivation was always financial. Although the Crusades and trade with the East helped build a solid commercial and banking class in Spain, expulsion of the Arabs (who developed the agricultural base) and the Jews (who composed a strong commercial class and educated elite) during the Inquisition had severely depleted the country's population, and with it the skills needed to sustain a developing economy.

During the next centuries, three successive wars with France and constant battles with Holland, Britain, and France for military superiority in the New World left Spain trying to consolidate the remainder of her European holdings and secure control of the Americas. A stubborn insistence on a Seville-controlled monopoly of all trade in the New World put Spain in constant conflict with European trading partners. At the same time, production of goods in her own mainland Latin American colonies undermined the market for domestic exports. Meanwhile, the Spanish monarchy continued to support an elitist, class-divided society. This was dominated by an immense nobility that monopolized power in the church and military, yet failed to convert enormous wealth from colonies such as Peru and Mexico into sustainable assets.

CUBA EMERGES

By the 1560s, the Spanish fleets had been consolidated, and Havana had become the official transit station for all ships traveling from the Americas to Cádiz. Cuba's strategic position on the Florida Straits and close proximity to such important South and Central American ports as Cartagena, Portobelo, and Veracruz made the island the most important of the Antilles. Yet, in a strange trick of fate, Cuba's future hinged not on her relationship to the richer South American colonies, but on her separateness from them.

After it became clear that the Caribbean islands would not be a great source of precious metals (copper and gold mining efforts in Cuba had peaked by the 1530s), the monarchy turned its sights to mineral-rich Mexico and Peru. These colonies developed diversified economies supported by a labor force drawn largely from an existing indigenous population. During its first century under Spanish rule Cuba also sustained a reasonably varied economy based on tobacco, shipbuilding and related mercantile trades, and exports of beef and hides, indigo, cotton, precious woods, and beeswax.

The island was never developed by Spain as a colony on its own, however. When Cuba did grow significantly for the first time in the late 1700s, it did so primarily with a one-crop economy—sugar—dependent on an imported work force—African slaves. Just as other possessions slipped away, the colony, once the poor second cousin, became Spain's most important source of income. The increasingly tight bond between the two was solidified in the 19th century by an influx of Spanish loyalists from former Latin American colonies and by Cuba's island geography, which made it more difficult for liberal ideas (and the *independistas* themselves) to flow in and out of the colony.

But it was slavery—critical to the Cuban economy as in no other Latin colony—that set the island apart. Around 1840, at the peak of the sugar boom, slaves numbered more than 400,000—almost one half of the entire population of the island, a statistic never remotely approached elsewhere in Latin America. A slave rebellion that ruined Haitian planters in 1791 had perpetuated fear of similar circumstances in Cuba. In the end, prolonged dependence on Spain was preferable to the unthinkable possibility that freedom for the Creole aristocracy might also bring freedom for slaves and equality between blacks and whites.

SEVEN CITIES

Cuba's early colonial history centers on the seven *villas* founded by the expeditionary Diego Velázquez de Cuéllar on behalf of the Spanish crown: Nuestra Señora de la Asunción de Baracoa (1512); San Salvador de Bayamo (1513); la Santísima Trinidad (1514); Sancti Spíritus

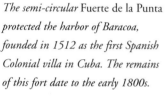

The semi-circular Fuerte de la Punta *protected the harbor of Baracoa, founded in 1512 as the first Spanish Colonial villa in Cuba. The remains of this fort date to the early 1800s.*

Due to pirate raids, the villa of Remedios was moved twice before being permanently established near Santa Clara in the 1570s. The location of the main square dates to that period.

(1514); Santa María del Puerto Príncipe, now Camagüey (1514); San Cristobal de la Habana (1514); and Santiago de Cuba (1515). (An eighth settlement, Santa Cruz de la Sabana, now San Juan de los Remedios del Cayo, was also established with a 1514 land grant, but had no municipal government.)

Proximity to gold and copper deposits, good coastal or river sites, and Arawak (sub-Taíno and Taíno) Indian settlements determined the sites of the first *villas,* which actually shifted from their original locations in virtually all cases. (Havana, for example, was moved in a series of steps from its original 1514 southern

Founded in 1515, Santiago occupies a series of hills near the Sierra Maestra in the heart of the Oriente Province. Buildings were adapted to the terraced topography, with rear rooms often situated at a lower level than front rooms.

CUBA: 400 YEARS OF ARCHITECTURAL HERITAGE

site near present-day Batabanó to its current north-coast location by 1519, while Puerto Príncipe was resituated from Nuevitas Bay to an interior Indian village in 1528. (The new village was located near fertile flatlands and safely away from pirate raids.)

The colonial *villas* became the nuclei for three distinct historical regions of the island, developed around differing cultures and economies. Of the three, eastern Cuba was traditionally the poorest and most provincial, with the most heterogeneous population and a mixed economy typically based on smaller family enterprises. The region included Cuba's first capital, Baracoa, an isolated fishing town; Camagüey, an important livestock center and later sugar capital; and Bayamo. This site of early gold mines was also a livestock region and an active smuggling point for French and Dutch contraband.

Then, as now, however, the most important eastern city was Santiago de Cuba, situated on the southeast coast in the heart of the Oriente region. From the start, Santiago was the island's melting pot, with a distinct mix of Spanish-born *peninsulares*, Creoles, blacks, Dominicans, and the thousands of French planters who poured in after the Haitian revolution of the 1790s. With its protected harbor, Santiago was the strategic starting point for expeditions in the conquest of Latin America. It was also the early seat of the bishopric and served as the Cuban administrative center from 1515–53.

Without an important capital city, central Cuba was left to develop more or less independently as the site of the island's most conservative, aristocratic cities. The southern port of Trinidad had important ties to Cartagena and served as a base for Cortés's conquest of Mexico. By the late 1700s, this elegant *villa*, along with Sancti Spíritus and Remedios, ranked among Cuba's most important sugar centers.

Havana dominated the western region of Cuba, always the most affluent and privileged. The city was the point of contact for all Gulf Stream traffic between Spain and the New World, and Spain's move to make the port its imperial outpost in the Caribbean consolidated the importance of the military, the church, and trade there. By 1750 about one half of the island's entire population (some 170,000) lived in the city, officially declared capital in 1607.

Early colonial Havana was a frontier town in the fullest sense, building an economic base on trades and services geared to the thousands of sailors stationed there for months at a time. Shipbuilding and construction were both important industries. By the early 18th century Havana had formed strong commercial contacts with the Gulf Coast, extending trade all the way up the Mississippi River and become the center for tobacco products that were by then Cuba's most important source of foreign income.

LAND GRANTS AND EARLY CITY PLANNING

The earliest settlers of Cuba's colonial towns and satellite agricultural and cattle settlements consisted primarily of two distinct groups that formed the basis for the colony's future class system. One group was peasant farmers and laborers, drawn largely from the Canary Islands (formally recognized as a Castilian possession in 1749) by land grants. The other sector of the population was the aristocracy, typically Castilian minor nobility, or *segundones* (second sons) from New Castile and Extremadura (southwest Spain).

The political and social makeup of Cuban towns was oligarchic, placing all power in the hands of a privileged few. Governing authority rested with the *cabildo*, essentially a de facto town council authorized by the Spanish governor, with membership limited to the Spanish-born *peninsulares*. The *cabildo* oversaw early distribution of property grants, or *mercedes*, which were directly related to class standing. The smallest parcels, known as *peónias*, went to peasant farmers. Substantial *caballerías* were awarded to privileged gentlemen, or *caballeros*, with the stipulation that the owners live in Cuba. These large land grants radiated in circles from a central point, where the owner was supposed to operate an inn, and where the heart of a small settlement inevitably formed. Even today, the roads and borders of many Cuban towns reflect this peculiar circular layout.

The design, siting, and layout of all Spanish colonial towns were subject to an important series of regulations, issued over many years and codified in 1573 as the New Laws of the Indies. The New Laws of the Indies actually derived from theological debate and were in theory intended to correct the moral transgressions associated with colonization, thus protecting the

The 1514 villa of Trinidad nestles in the foothills of the Escambray mountains. A town ordinance prescribed a daily schedule for throwing waste water into the stone-paved streets, where a central channel was designed to keep all water away from house foundations.

CUBA: 400 YEARS OF ARCHITECTURAL HERITAGE

rights of native populations. In practice, however, they served as an instrument of the state to control nearly every aspect of colonial life.

Among the objects of rules were street width and orientation, exterior paint colors for buildings, and the size and configuration of blocks and plazas. These were to be laid out in a strict grid based on the layout of a Roman military camp and intended to impose both physical and psychological order. As now, the plaza was the vital heart of the city, and in the colonial era an extremely important center for political, military, commercial, and social activity. This central space not only housed municipal buildings, private *palacios,* shops, and market stalls, but also served as a setting for military parades, fiestas, medieval jousts—and, not incidentally, public executions.

Dimensions for the plaza were remarkably specific: It was to be rectangular, with the four corners aligned with the compass points; the minimum size was set at 200 x 300 feet, with one side always one-and-a-half times as long as the other. Two streets were to meet at right angles at each corner and four more to lead out from the center of each side to make it easy for cavalry parades to pass through. Buildings were

also supposed to incorporate *portales,* or shaded arcades "for the convenience of merchants," but until the 1700s few Cuban towns actually complied, mainly in order to cut costs.

The 16th-century *Plaza de Armas* in Havana, (which originally occupied part of the site of the *Castillo de la Real Fuerza*), was the city's first plaza, and served as the nucleus for a grid plan that clearly defines Old Havana today. It is important to note, however, that the New Laws of the Indies were ignored as often as they were honored. While cities founded from the mid-1600s onward, including Santa Clara, Matanzas, and Holguín, generally followed legal norms of design *"a regla y cordel,"* many of the early colonial towns did not. Camagüey, Bayamo, and Sancti Spíritus incorporated plazas, but still had irregular plans of winding streets more medieval than Renaissance in character. Trinidad and Santiago developed semi-regular grids with few if any true square blocks. Santiago is remarkable for its natural adaptation to a series of terraced hills rising from the bay. The plan comprises a system of plazas moving from east to west, with the city spreading from the harbor in rings of graduated levels so that it resembles an oversized amphitheater.

Although the Plaza Vieja *in Old Havana was established in the 1500s, the existing Creole palaces fronted by arched* portales *were built a century later. This plaza is unusual in that it was entirely residential.*

The enclosed patio (right) and the central town plaza (below) were integral components of early Cuban urban life. An iron fence and classical urns were added to Trinidad's plaza in the 1800s to give the town square a more fashionable classical aspect.

Exterior decorative painting, like the murals on the Casa del Conde de Casa Lombillo *in Havana, was widespread in colonial Cuba.*

CUBA: 400 YEARS OF ARCHITECTURAL HERITAGE

THE FORT

Of the three fundamental pillars of early Cuban society—the military, the Church, and the *cabildo,* the military was most important. Formal plans for fortifications in the Caribbean were consolidated during the reigns of Charles I (1516–56) and Philip II (1556–98) and expanded by successive rulers over the next centuries. The first line of defense was strictly military and consisted of coastal forts situated at strategic points around the circumference of the island; set on a high promontory, or *morro,* the forts were designed to command views of water and land approaches alike. As towns grew in importance so, logically, did their fortification systems; by the 19th century these became as critical to protecting the colonial interests of important sugar towns like Trinidad from internal attack from Cuban revolutionaries during the independence wars as they had been against European navies in the centuries before.

While they were impressive engineering accomplishments, these fortification projects were characteristically plagued by administrative problems. Massive military constructions were a constant drain on finances and funding for early forts had to come from the budget for Mexico. As a result, wages were erratic, late, and often inadequate. Rebellions and infighting among workers sometimes resulted in inferior work and even defects in the finished projects.

Military engineers nevertheless earned great professional esteem and their technical skills did build them deserved reputations. Among the first-known European military engineers to work on the island was one Bartolomé Sánchez, who worked on the *Castillo Real Fuerza,* considered to be the oldest stone fort in the Americas. Set adjacent to the *Plaza de Armas* at the mouth of the Havana bay, the *Castillo* was com-

Because of the main plaza's military and commercial role in early colonial Cuba, the New Laws of the Indies required that the central square be located near a harbor. Remodeled in the 1700s, Havana's Plaza de Armas *was permanently established as a civic center in the 1580s. Like all early colonial Cuban plazas, it was originally treeless.*

Ironworks for constructing the Castillo de la Real Fuerza *in Havana were established in 1558 and the first stones laid in 1562. The fort was designed by Bartolomé Sánchez and Francisco de Calona. Slaves and French prisoners were used for labor.*

missioned in 1558 to replace an earlier fort destroyed by French Corsairs three years earlier. It was executed, as was customary, in collaboration with the city's *maestro mayor,* or master planner, then Francisco de Calona.

The best-known military engineers in early colonial Cuba, however, were members of an illustrious Milanese family named Antonelli. Beginning in 1581, Bautista Antonelli, the family patriarch, was responsible for an extensive Latin American fortification system encompassing projects in Vera Cruz, Portobelo, Cartagena, and elsewhere in the Caribbean. Antonelli arrived in Havana in 1589 at the order of Philip II to take over the *Zanja Real* aqueduct. With his nephew Cristóbal de Roda, he built both the *Castillo de San Salvador de la Punta* (1589–1600) and the *Castillo de los Tres Reyes del Morro* (1589–1630), two extremely important forts strategically paired to close off the entrance canal to the bay of Havana.

Characteristic of the era, Antonelli's designs were based on a type of European fortification developed after the advent of gunpowder in the late Middle Ages and refined in the early Renaissance. The rigidly symmetrical plan incorporated an interior plaza containing barracks, dungeons, powder stores, a treasury, officers' and troop quarters, and a chapel. A complex system of moats and passages and battered masonry walls augmented with pointed bulwarks to counter artillery fire shored up the defenses.

In 1607, the island administration was divided into two departments—one in Havana, the other in Santiago—in an attempt to reduce smuggling and improve coastal surveillance. At this time, Juan Bautista Antonelli, the son of Bautista Antonelli, was charged with overhauling the defense system in Santiago and began work on the *Castillo de San Pedro de la Roca* (known as the *Castillo del Morro*) in 1639. This fort is particularly notable for its adaptation to its terraced site at the top of a steep promontory, or *morro,* at the head of the bay. The design incorporates three bulwarks and four main levels connected by stairs; supplies were delivered by water to the bottom level where an artillery warehouse was dug directly into the cliffs. Called back to Havana, Juan Bautista Antonelli was also responsible for at least two additional twin forts, the *Fuerte de Cojímar* (c. 1645) and the *Fuerte de Santa Dorotea de Luna de la Chorrera* (c. 1645). Both were intended to protect the Cojímar and Almendares Rivers (respectively located east and west of Havana) and cut off potential attackers from fresh-water supplies.

Santiago's 1639 Castillo del Morro, designed by the military engineer Juan Bautista Antonelli, was perfectly situated above the mouth of the bay.

Juan Bautista's small Fuerte de Cojímar *(right), built circa 1645 at the mouth of the Cojímar River in eastern Havana, measures eighteen meters square and contained quarters for a commander and his infantry, as well as a chapel. Juan Bautista's father, the Italian military engineer Bautista Antonelli, designed Havana's* Castillo de los Tres Reyes del Morro *(below) in 1589.*

THE CHURCH

Cultivating music and theater, the Catholic Church was the basis of cultural as well as religious life and the foundation for the first educational institutions. Before a university was founded in Havana in 1728 (a monastic institution that was secularized in 1841), the seminaries offered the only higher education available in the colony. The earliest of these were in Havana; the 1722 *Seminario de San Basilio* in Santiago was the first institution for higher education in the eastern province of Oriente. (The first public school in Cuba was not established until 1788, and this too, was the project of a Catholic priest.)

In order to establish a village, it was necessary to have a church; without one, the Crown would not provide the funds for the town. On a few occasions, specific groups of colonizers were required to emigrate to Cuba from the Canary Islands to start towns. There were five of these *ciudades sufragáneas* (which required a minimum of thirty families) in Cuba: Bejucal, Santa María del Rosario, Jaruco, San Antonio de los Baños, and Guantánamo. Some of the new Cuban settlements were feuds, or land distributions, to noblemen who would add this *señorío* to their name (as in the Lord of Jaruco, or the Marquis of San Felipe and Santiago). Such noblemen served as patrons of the town, funding its church and often maintaining a summer residence there.

The Church was an important economic force and its early monastic orders sometimes amassed considerable wealth. (A 1762 guide prepared for English visitors to Havana even went so far as to cite the "rich" Dominican monastery and nunnery of Santa Catalina, and the "very, very rich" Franciscan monastery.) Heavy tithes required of local farmers filled the ecclesiastical coffers. To ensure eternal salvation, parishioners were also encouraged to bequeath their property to monasteries, which became major landowners. Convents, in turn, exacted considerable dowries from novices; an entire house, the *Casa del Marino,* tucked into a secondary cloister of the Convent of Santa Clara de Asís in Havana, was part of such a dowry. Novices usually came from the aristocracy and typically entered a convent accompanied by a slave.

The first cathedral on the island was founded in Baracoa, and a second at Bayamo. Santiago's cathedral was established around 1523 and Camagüey's around 1530; many

The early baroque church of the Convent of Santo Domingo in Guanabacoa was designed in 1730 by Lorenzo Camacho. The symmetrical facade is divided into three vertical bays, reflecting a three-nave interior plan.

The 1675 Ermita del Potosi *in Guanabacoa (right) and* La Popa *in Trinidad (below) are examples of the small single-room Cuban* ermitas *that were remodeled in subsequent centuries.*

The order of San Francisco de Asís was founded in 1563 in Havana and the church erected in the 1730s on the site of an earlier ermita. *The tower was added later in the century.*

towns followed as their size and importance merited a bishopric. The most important church aside from the cathedral was the *parroquial mayor,* the temple to the holy spirit (*espíritu santo*) and the seat of the highest priest in the region. The status of the *parroquial mayor* merited a prominent location on the side or corner of the town's main plaza and by the early 1700s, it was not unusual for it to occupy an entire block. The church often incorporated a monastery or convent, although these would be phased out after the liberal legislation of the 1830s. The self-contained complex of *Santa Clara de Asís,* begun in Havana in 1638, for example, which incorporated three separate cloisters (two now restored) and a single-nave church, occupied four city blocks.

Ermitas, or hermitages, were also an important part of Cuban culture. A tradition dating back to the 1500s, these were simple neighborhood churches to which a preacher came only on the day of the mass; worshipers traditionally brought seats from home. As a town grew and a parish became wealthier, the *ermita* was often replaced by a more substantial church building, and many parish churches standing today have roots in these humble places of worship.

No matter what the type, the first Cuban churches, including the cathedrals, were rudimentary structures with walls of wood plank or an adobe-like mud mixture called *embarrado,* and thatched *guano* (palm) roofs. These were gradually replaced by more substantial stone buildings with a tile or wood roof and simple rectangular plan. Beginning around 1600, the single-nave plan with a chancel at the end was introduced, perhaps the influence of the first Cartagena cathedral (1593), which was widely imitated in northern Latin America. As funds permitted, churches were customarily enlarged with new designs that often incorporated the old structure. The cruciform plan separated from side aisles with arched piers (as in the church of *San Francisco de Asís* in Havana) and distinguished by unusual barrel vaults, probably appeared in the 1700s.

By the 18th century, the Cuban church facade typically revealed the characteristic features of Spanish baroque ecclesiastical design. The wall plane, which gained shadow-catching surface relief from engaged columns and shallow niches, was broken into two or three horizontal levels by continuing cornice lines and crowned with a curving pediment; there might be one or

THE EARLY COLONIAL ERA

The plan of the Church of San Francisco de Asís in Havana comprises a central nave with two side aisles. The interior is notable for arched lateral vaults that intersect with the nave, resulting in barrel-like dormers.

The Churrigueresque-style altar of the 17th-century parroquial mayor *of San Juan Bautista in Remedios was carved of cedar and encrusted with gold leaf. A reaction against Protestantism, the Spanish baroque exalted the Eucharist and saints with ornate iconography. Gold symbolized divine light, and fruit represented the bounty of God-given life.*

two lateral towers. *Il Gesú* in Rome (1568–84), the mother church of the Jesuits, is widely cited as the distant ancestor of this basic scheme, which was echoed and redefined over the next centuries in Catholic countries, especially in Latin America. The variations on church design, however, were countless and diffused; monasteries, in particular, were founded by orders from all over Spain, and showed a variety of regional influences. The hand of the Mudéjar craftsman from Andalusia in southern Spain is evidenced in Cuba's parish churches by the widespread use of hand-pieced *alfarjes* (wood ceilings) with prism-patterned *tirantes* (cross beams). Elaborate carved and gilded altars, *retablos,* and pulpits in the Churrigueresque tradition also appeared in towns throughout the island during the first half of the 18th century.

The Church of Santo Domingo in Guanabacoa was designed by Lorenzo Camacho in 1728 and constructed by artisans from the Canary Islands. The alfarje *is one of the most complicated in colonial Cuba; no nails were used for the design, which comprizes thousands of fitted wood pieces.*

THE HOUSE

Early colonial domestic architecture in Cuba traced a slow but logical progression of development. Houses throughout the island shared typological similarities—most notably the Mudéjar-inspired interior patio—but there were also many regional variations in plan and detail, shaped in part by differing climates and topography. Sixteenth-century Cuba was a colony in transition and architecture was temporary in every sense. Houses were quite literally built for the moment; most people were waiting to move on to something better.

The first colonial buildings borrowed directly from native Arawak Indian traditions. Early houses were simple huts modeled on the sub-Taíno *bohío,* a simple one-room structure with walls sheathed with plank-like *yaguas* made

High narrow stairways called pretorios *are indigenous to cities such as Santiago. Earlier in this century, many were truncated or removed altogether when streets were widened to accommodate automobiles.*

Urns, or copas, *were used to embellish rooftops throughout the island. These 19th-century examples on an early colonial house in Guanabacoa are among the only originals left in Cuba.*

CUBA: 400 YEARS OF ARCHITECTURAL HERITAGE

Truncated pilasters and projecting turned-wood roof brackets called turnapuntas *are regional features of Camagüey. Such roof brackets were outlawed as unfashionable in the mid-1800s.*

The multi-curved arco mixtilíneo (right) is indigenous to the architecture of Camagüey. The mirador *house (bottom), characterized by a full second-story balcony, is an 18th-century colonial type found in Santiago.*

CUBA: 400 YEARS OF ARCHITECTURAL HERITAGE

from the upper bark of the palm tree and a waterproof palm-thatch roof; to this basic scheme the Spanish added windows and a porch. *Bohíos* were scattered through the countryside (tidy versions are still common today) but were also ubiquitous in cities, where they were typically clustered in slum-like neighborhoods on the outskirts. The urban *bohío* neighborhoods became such a problem that a ban was issued in Havana as early as 1571, although it evidently didn't work as they continued to proliferate.

In the area of Santiago de Cuba, frequent earthquakes led to the adoption of traditional Indian pole-frame construction in which vertical supports of an extremely hard wood such as *jiquí, ácana* (ironwood), or *chicharrón* (pig-

wood) were driven directly into the ground, then entwined with flexible withes of *cuje*, a native cane fiber, and plastered with a lime mixture. When a tremor hit, the plaster would crumble, but the framework would stand.

In addition to variations on *cuje* construction, houses were also built of *embarrado*. These simple thatched roofed buildings were gradually replaced by those of a more substantial *mampostería*, a combination of brick and crushed soft limestone. Beginning around the late 16th century *mampostería* houses with wood shingle or clay tile roofs became increasingly prevalent, particularly in Sancti Spíritus, Trinidad, and Camagüey as various technologies developed around the island.

The restored Casa de Diego Velázquez de Cuellar *recreates the Moorish-style house the Spanish conquistador built in Santiago in the first half of the 1500s. Family rooms were on this second-story gallery, which opens onto an inner patio.*

Cuje *construction of fiber and mud (right) was one of the earliest building methods used by Spanish settlers. The vertical poles were singed on the ends to produce a water-resistant charcoal layer, then driven directly into the soil.* Bohios *like these guano-thatched houses in Las Villas (below) are based on Arawak Indian dwellings and have been used in Cuba since the 1500s.*

The Mudéjar patio plan, the nucleus of the colonial Cuban house, probably began to be used in the early 17th century as settlers adopted more sophisticated designs and built more permanent structures. The enclosed open-air patio was directly derivative of the medieval Arabic tradition of a private inner court where women were cloistered and most domestic activities occurred. Its introduction in Cuba was important in that it signaled the first transition from a primitive one-room plan to a layout that designated specific uses to specific spaces. The patio was also a necessary means of ventilation for contiguous houses that shared bearing walls.

The fundamental concept of the patio plan depended on a hierarchy of rooms (with graduated size and ceiling heights) moving from public and formal to casual and private. At the front was the best *sala,* generally a showplace for furniture, and one or two *aposentos,* or bedrooms, with a smaller *saleta* and flanking *recámaras* (less important bedrooms) located directly to the

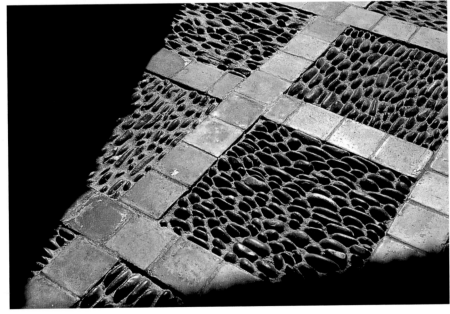

Crumbling plaster reveals mamposteria *of rubble and brick (top). A patio floor is paved with river stones known as* chinas pelonas, *or "bald stones" (above).*

A central element of the colonial courtyard was the well. Most early colonial Cuban houses had a drainpipe system that collected rainwater from the channels running between rows of roof tiles, and directed it to an underground cistern.

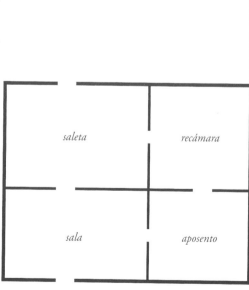

Early Colonial House

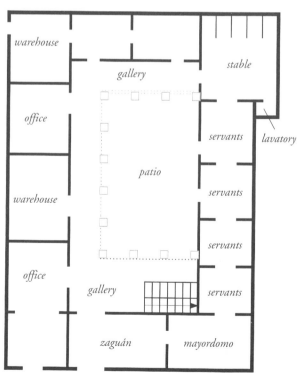

Havana House, first floor

rear. As the plan evolved according to changing social patterns, a rear gallery, used for sewing, reading, and dining, was added, opening onto an enlarged patio landscaped with shade trees and potted plants. This was enclosed by a U- or L-shaped wing of smaller contiguous rooms, including sleeping quarters, bath, and kitchen. There might be trading areas to sell farm products on one side of the ground floor.

The vast majority of early colonial houses were limited to one story, due in part to economics and in part to earthquakes. In some instances a single second-story room (used as an office or library) was located over a front corner; this has been preserved in a few extant 17th-century houses in Havana, and was adopted for 18th-century planters' houses in some sugar centers, such as Trinidad.

The exception to the rule was Havana, where two-story *palacios* were built around the important plazas and their ancillary streets. One reason for this was a space shortage that eventually made taller buildings compulsory; moreover, Havana was not threatened by earthquakes. And the other reason was money. The grand Havana house plan was the perfect expression of the hierarchy of privilege accorded to members of an upper-class *habanero* household. Opening directly from the street was a private enclosed *zaguán,* or gateway, where large doors permitted carriages to pass through into the patio. In a scheme seldom found outside of the capital city, the ground-floor rooms, distributed down one or both sides of the court, were devoted to warehouses, offices, and other services connected to the family business; servants' rooms and stables were located in the rear. Reached by a private inner stair, the family quarters were secluded on the galleried second story.

Particularly distinctive to this Havana plan was the *entresuelo,* a kind of mezzanine tucked between the two floors, a feature brought from such bay area Andalusian towns as Jerez and Cádiz. The *entresuelo,* which housed slaves and servants (and was sometimes rented out) was first added to existing structures by stealing space from the ground floor (hence its half-story proportions). By the mid-1700s, however, it had become an integral part of the house design from its inception.

In the medieval tradition of the Moors, early Cuban houses were built in a contiguous

line with common bearing walls, or *medianeras.* Crowned with pitched or hipped roofs, their flat, plain facades fronted directly on the street in an almost fortress-like manner. In addition to the patio, many Mudéjar elements influenced house design well into the 18th century. Most notable was the use of deep-set windows with turned-wood window grates, or *rejas;* hanging balconies (on two-story houses); and clay barrel roof tiles. Inside the house, the hand of the Mudéjar artisan was also evident in such distinctive features as the intricate wooden *alfarjes,* paneled doors, and decorated ceramic floor tiles.

The one-story Santiago house called the fachada simple *(top) shared party walls with contiguous dwellings; the courtyard was located inside. Some early Camagüey houses had a triangular plan (above).*

The two-story Havana plan with central courtyard, entresuelo, *and side stairs is exemplified by the 1720* Casa del Conde de Bayona *in Old Havana (right and below).*

The influence of the Spanish baroque appears to have reached Havana by the late 1600s, as evidenced by the elaborate, sculptural stone door enframement distinguishing the *Casa de la Obra Pía*. The stonework was crafted in Spain around 1686, then shipped to Havana. Elements from both the Mudéjar and baroque traditions, however, were widely mixed until the late 1700s, when the baroque reached its full flowering.

The Casa del Conde de San Juan Jaruco *in Havana, with an interior gallery supported by stone columns, was rebuilt in 1737 from remnants of an earlier 18th-century house.*

Part III

THE LATE COLONIAL ERA

1762–1898

*An infinite variety of deco-
rative patterns brought texture and variety to the
columns of the shade-giving
portal, which remained an
integral element of Cuban
architecture throughout the
late colonial era.*

By contrast to the relatively slow pace of growth during the first 250 years of Spanish settlement, the late colonial era unfolded in rapid layers of change. Although brief, the ten-month British occupation of Havana in 1762 during the Seven Years' War precipitated two developments with major implications: access to the lucrative English slave trade and a temporary but important break in Spain's trade monopoly. Both cast light on Cuba's potential as a player in international economics, and soon after British forces departed, the island shed its role as service colony to become the world's premier sugar producer. Indeed, before the late 19th-century independence wars plunged the economy into ruin, Cuba would emerge the richest colony in the New World—likely richer than Spain herself.

During the late 1700s, the effects of Bourbon reforms also began to filter into the Hispano-Caribbean region under the reign of Charles III (1759–88). The new king saw an efficiently managed colonial empire in the Indies as the key to imperial prosperity for an increasingly bankrupt monarchy. Spain again deployed European military engineers to shore up Caribbean defenses and while administrative controls tightened, trade regulations were actually liberalized to stimulate agricultural and commercial development. This, in turn, set the stage for a Creole reformist movement that became the foundation for an unprecedented period of intellectual and economic advances in Cuba, as a thriving free-enterprise system sustained a constant flow of new opportunities.

Both the climate of enlightenment and the concomitant economic progress owed much to the *Sociedad Económica de Amigos del País,* an influential cultural and civic organization for learning and debate chartered in 1793 by Havana's leading Creole intelligentsia. Under the stewardship of Francisco de Arango y Parreño, a prominent economist, the Sociedad redirected the focus of life to *Cuban*—rather than Spanish—concerns in the interest of making the island a showcase of achievement. Members promoted the sciences, education, and the arts (it was the Sociedad that commissioned Jean Baptiste Vermay as head of the academy of *bellas artes*) and won critical concessions on behalf of Creole sugar planters. In a move that would revolutionize the sugar industry, the Sociedad brought the first steam-powered *ingenio,* or sugar mill, to Cuba (purchased in London in 1794), and was instrumental in building the 1837 railroad. This was the first railroad in Latin America, founded before even Spain herself inaugurated a rail system.

A spread of rationalist ideas and Freemasonry (introduced during British occupation) also informed an increasingly secular society. The organization of a secular university in 1841 marked a break with the Spanish ecclesiastical tradition; complementing the old, conservative

Located in the Valle de los Ingenios, the 18th-century Ingenio Manacas belonged to the Hernández de Iznaga family, which also owned several townhouses in Trinidad. The formal garden was typical of these country palacetes.

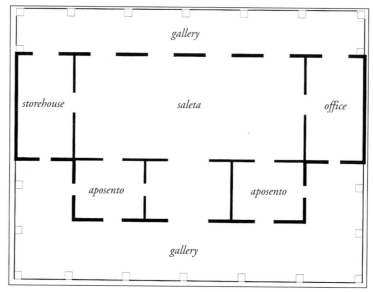

Ingenio

CUBA: 400 YEARS OF ARCHITECTURAL HERITAGE

curriculum of theology, mathematics, and law were new courses in philosophy, as well as political science, economics, and botany. All these subjects were directly relevant to agricultural production.

Just as the cultural enlightenment heightened awareness of internal issues, increased foreign exchanges opened Cuba outward. With the increasing tide of European merchants and French and Spanish entrepreneurs from Louisiana came a flow of foreign periodicals and mail-order catalogues, along with new ideas, new materials, and new building technologies that would dramatically change the Cuban landscape. Although Creole reformists never wavered in their support of slavery, there was a strong solidarity with the ideas of the French Revolution, with the progressive nature of 19th-century French culture in general, and with French neoclassicism in particular. Cubans traveling abroad brought back French books, French wine, French music. It was the French who introduced photography and cinema to the island; even the best and fanciest prostitutes, it is said, were always French.

A NEW ECONOMY

Cuba's stupendous growth in sugar production during the late 18th and early 19th centuries was the collective result of several factors. These included a new market in Spain and the newly independent United States, the opening of Spanish ports to colonial trade, and meteoric price rises precipitated by the 1791 Haitian slave uprising, which destroyed the French sugar trade (formerly three quarters of the European market). The number of sugar mills soared. In 1700 there were about 100 rudimentary *trapiches* (ox- or mule-powered mills) located mostly around Havana. By the early 1800s the total was about 500 island wide, many of which were modernized steam-powered *ingenios*. By 1846 the number of mills surged to about 1440. Annual sugar production exploded from 14,000 tons in 1790 to 34,000 tons in 1805.

Sugar was king, but Cuban progress also depended in part on coffee and tobacco. In the 1790s, coffee cultivation, introduced to Cuba in the 1760s, spread rapidly across the island. This was especially true in the east, where

A paved secadero, *for drying coffee beans, fronts the* cafetal La Isabelica *in la Granpiedra, located in the mountains near Santiago. Most of the Cuban* cafetales *in Oriente were burned during the Independence Wars because they were so critical to the economic foundation of the area.*

The interior of La Isabelica *shows the* saleta *and adjacent bedroom, or* aposento, *which opened directly off the main living space in a layout similar to that of the Cuban sugar plantation.*

French planters from Haiti established hundreds of coffee estates, or *cafetales,* creating their own paradise in the mountains around Santiago and Guantánamo. Coffee cultivation was a vital industry until devastating hurricanes and high U.S. tariffs seriously damaged production in the 1840s. The industry was further slowed by competition from Brazil and by the Ten Years' War. Tobacco production, concentrated in the western areas of Pinar del Río and Viñales, fared better, but prices were also subject to the vagaries of tariff wars.

The sugar mills and the *cafetales* were the core of civilization in the Cuban countryside, the setting for a court-like salon culture of music, theater, philosophy and letters, art, and French cuisine that also transformed the island's important cities by the early 1800s. By contrast to the coffee planters, who lived on their plantations full-time, sugar planters helped strengthen the link between the plantations and sugar capitals by maintaining elegant *palacios* in town and residing at the plantations only on weekends.

Set up like towns, plantations ranged from about 100 to 1000 acres in size and consisted of numerous buildings known collectively as a *batey,* an Indian word for the plaza at the center of Arawak villages. Among these buildings were the main *casa de vivienda* or *palacete;* lodgings for the administrator and white salaried employees; slave barracks; the *ingenio,* where the cane was milled; the *casa de purga* for clarifying the *guarapo* (cane syrup); infirmary; kitchen; stables; warehouses; and one or more rail stops.

The *cafetales* also comprised impressive complexes with separate drying ovens, kitchen, and *tahona,* or crushing mill, a two-story house with living quarters set over warehouses and an adjacent *secadero,* or drying terrace. While coffee planters typically adopted Spanish building traditions in town, the *cafetales* were more characteristically European, often approached by elegant tree-lined drives and gardens planted in the French tradition with formal flower beds and fruit trees.

NEW CITIES

Soaring agricultural production and an exploding slave population supporting it created a kind of double geography: the rural plantations (owned by Creole elites) and the cities that supplied them through a growing class of merchants and moneylenders (primarily Spanish *peninsulares* who dominated Cuban commerce).

By the mid-1800s, cultivation of sugar cane had expanded, moving south from Havana into western Cuba, east along the north coast, down through the center of the island, and, to a lesser degree, to the east around Holguín, Bayamo, Guantánamo, and Santiago. On the south coast, Trinidad, which exported one third of the island's sugar from some fifty-six mills in the nearby Valle de los Ingenios during the peak years, became the third most important city in Cuba after Havana and Santiago. Trinidad traded directly with Europe, South America, the United States, and Spain. Matanzas, about 100 kilometers east of Havana on the north coast, became the largest sugar exporter in the world by the mid-19th century and a magnet for some of Cuba's most prominent scientists and literati of the era.

Progressive merchants and slave owners initiated plans for entirely new towns as well. More than fifty new cities were started between 1795 and 1840. Among the most prosperous were Guantánamo (established in 1797 and a center for *ingenios* by about 1820); Cienfuegos (originally Fernandina de Jagua, founded in 1819 by Louis de Clouet, a Creole trader from New Orleans); and Cárdenas (1828), with a well-situated harbor about thirty miles east of Matanzas. Regla, across the harbor from Havana, became an important sugar port and Güines a terminal for the first Havana railroad. A fashion for medicinal baths among French travelers and the better layers of Cuban society also transformed other towns, such as Guanabacoa, Puentes Grandes, and San Antonio de los Baños—all rich in mineral waters—into popular holiday spas where old *palacios* were redesigned as elegant hotels.

The Iznaga Tower commands a view across the 250-square-kilometer Valle de los Ingenios, once a major center for sugar mills near Trinidad. By the early 1900s, only one mill in the valley was still operating; some seventy ruins remain today.

A NEW URBANISM

In a pattern consistently repeated by successive leaders, late-Colonial Cuba was the object of repeated urban renewal plans intended to shape a powerful public face for the island. With the return of Spanish power in Havana in 1763, an immediate program for Havana began under Felipe de Fonsdeviela, the Marqués de la Torre. The period heralded a new emphasis on public works. The governor's plan called for the redesign of the old city squares, including the *Plaza de Armas,* and introduced such improvements as street lighting and sidewalks; it also included the first grand public theater in Cuba, and the first major avenue outside Havana city walls, the *Paseo de Extramuros* (later renamed *Paseo de Isabel II,* then *Paseo del Prado,* and now officially *Paseo de Martí*).

During the late 1700s, a trio of important military engineers—Pedro Medina, a native of Cadiz; Silvestre Abarca, Brigadeer of Engineers and eventual *maestro mayor* of Havana; and Cuban-born Antonio Fernández de Trevejos, Lt. Colonel of Engineers—reconstructed Havana's defense system. In various combinations, the three worked on the new forts of *San Carlos de la Cabaña* (1763–64) above the entrance to the inner harbor, the *Castillo de Santo Domingo de Atarés* (1767), and the *Castillo del Príncipe* (1767–79).

With the growth of old cities and the birth of new ones came a more comprehensive approach to 19th-century urban planning. This reinforced the grid advised by the New Laws of the Indies, but now endowed it with a sense of ceremony and formal monumentality in a contextual approach to architecture and planning at least partly derivative of European models. Broad, landscaped boulevards punctuated with formal statuary created definitive axes, while classically inspired public buildings brought a new scale to enlarged plazas. These influences were particularly clear in the plan for Cienfuegos, conceived as a whole in 1819, and settled by a colony of French planters from Louisiana. The design, which recalls that of New Orleans, incorporates a central boulevard with a formally landscaped median, a precise grid of 100-hectare square blocks and parks, and an enormous *Plaza de Armas* covering two full blocks, unusual for a Cuban city.

In the same spirit, Havana was again transformed under Captain-General Miguel Tacón (1834–38), an ultra-conservative monarchist who conceived an integrated urban expansion designed to express a new sense of order in the colony. Executed by the military engineer Mariano Carrillo de Albornoz, Tacón's plan created a unified streetscape, setting the pace for other Cuban cities. Old facades were realigned and set to the rhythmic cadence of columned *portales* running for blocks at a time. The grand *Teatro Tacón* (twice reconstructed and finally incorporated into the *Centro Gallego*), fronted by a solid neoclassical portico, and the city's first railroad station were erected on the *Paseo de Extramuros.*

The crowning element was the *Prado Militar* (later named *Avenida Carlos III,* now *Avenida Salvador Allende*) knifing east/west across the city, intended to allow troops to enter Havana rapidly from the *Castillo del Príncipe* in case of revolt. This broad, straight boulevard not only accommodated cavalry parades (a ceremonial canon shot could be aimed straight down its length), but was also an expression of upper-class power. It served as a highly visible promenade for the occupants of the fashionable villas in the area of the *Quinta de los Molinos,* the governmental country house commissioned by Tacón in 1837.

To escape the densely populated city centers, affluent Cuban families had, in fact, begun drifting to city outskirts in search of healthier living conditions in the early 1800s. The expansion of *extramuros* residential districts, beginning with Havana's El Cerro—developed southwest of the old city between 1803 and the 1840s—marked the increased segregation of the classes. As open areas outside of Cuban cities were gradually built up with spacious freestanding *quintas,* or country villas, the abandoned inner-city *palacios* disintegrated into slums called *cuarterías.* By mid-century, cramped low-class rental buildings known as *solares* or *ciudadelas* began to proliferate.

In 1861, Cuba's first formal building codes, the *Ordenanzas de Construccion para la Ciudad de la Habana y los Pueblos de su Termino Municipal,* were passed, requiring proper professional credentials and legal permits for building or altering structures. The codes also prescribed compulsory *portales* for the avenues of *Calzada*

By the turn of the 19th century, balustrades began to appear atop the traditional Cuban portal. The inner patio of this Remedios house is visible from above.

The two-story freestanding quinta *began to appear in the early 1800s. An example in Rancho Boyeros (right) incorporates shaded galleries. The* Quinta de los Molinos *in Havana (below) was designed in 1837 by Félix Lemau and Manuel Pastor, who were commissioned by the governor Miguel Tacón to create an official summer residence on the fashionable Avenida Carlos III.*

CUBA: 400 YEARS OF ARCHITECTURAL HERITAGE

de la Reina and *El Prado*. The same year, a master plan by the engineer Francisco José de Albear y Lara, director of Cuba's Office of Public Works, called for the demolition of the city walls and traced new *ensanches,* or expansion districts, with double-width public avenues intersecting a grid of narrower private residential streets. Albear also proposed *chaflanes* (cutaway street corners) for some new Havana squares designed to open up tight spaces and promote better traffic circulation. This detail strongly suggests the influence of the 1857 *ensanche* plan for Madrid by Carlos María Castro and an 1859 design by Ildefons Cerdá,[1] the pioneer of modern planning in Barcelona; Albear himself had worked on a Barcelona city plan in 1846.

Urban green spaces, including public parks and botanical gardens, were also introduced during this period. The Havana suburb of Vedado, laid out in 1859, was the first city district to incorporate strips of planted greenery between sidewalk and street. Most Cuban cities gained a *parque republicano.* This was a block-sized park (often remodeled from an older plaza) designed as a precise rectangle. It was bisected with paths—often on a diagonal—punctuated with a fountain or statue at their intersection.

CIVIC ARCHITECTURE

Cuba's grand tradition of late-colonial civic architecture began with the 18th-century monuments the Marqués de la Torre commissioned for Havana's *Plaza de Armas.* Defining the remodeled square as the capital's administrative center are two of four civic buildings originally planned: the *Palacio del Segundo Cabo,* also known as the *Real Casa de Correos,* designed by the military engineer Antonio Fernández de Trevejos, and the *Palacio de los Capitanes Generales,* official seat of the colonial governors de-

The main square of Remedios was landscaped as a parque republicano *with a pavilion placed at the intersection of symmetrical paths.*

The Palacio del Segundo Cabo *(top) and the adjacent* Palacio de los Capitanes Generales *(above and right) were constructed in the 1790s to give Havana's* Plaza de Armas *a new monumental civic profile. Both buildings were designed by military engineers and epitomize the Cuban sense of baroque grandeur, which peaked in the late 1700s.*

El Templete, *situated directly across from the baroque* Palacio de los Capitanes Generales *on the* Plaza de Armas *in Havana is one of the oldest extant classical buildings in Cuba. The temple-fronted commemorative monument by Antonio María de la Torre was completed in 1828.*

signed by de Trevejos and Pedro Medina. These buildings were vivid expressions of the power of the monarchy, and still rank among the most important public buildings in Cuba. Both coral-stone structures, completed around 1791, incorporated the traditional central patio (that of the *Palacio de los Capitanes Generales* was enlarged in 1835), *entresuelo* and *portales* fronting

the plaza. Although larger, the *Palacio de los Capitanes Generales,* was intended to complement the design of its neighbor, (begun about seven years earlier). Then, the shared symmetry of the two buildings' rhythmic bays, arched *portales,* and ornate baroque window moldings with colored-glass transoms was immediately apparent and provided a sense of authoritative "correctness" to the cityscape.

The 1828 completion of *El Templete,* designed by Antonio María de la Torre for the south side of the *Plaza de Armas,* marked a new era of classically inspired public architecture that flourished in Cuban cities both large and small. Located directly opposite the *Palacio de los Capitanes Generales,* the small monument commemorated the spot where the first mass in Havana had been celebrated in the 16th century. Although this elegant structure was diminutive by comparison to the earlier municipal buildings it faces, its Greco-Roman temple front—a Doric portico supported a classical frieze of triglyphs and metopes and a full triangular pediment—gave it a distinct monumental order. Moreover, the composition represented a clean break with Mudéjar and Spanish baroque traditions and a firm alliance with French neoclassicism that would have a major influence on building design throughout the island for the next century.

El Templete was among the first of countless Cuban public structures that came hand in hand with improved commerce and transportation, the new focus on public works, and cultural, educational, and leisure development—including customs houses, railroad stations, markets, libraries, theaters, social and cultural clubs known as *casinos,* and even bullfighting rings. With few exceptions, this public architecture relied on the neoclassical style to convey a sense of cultural achievement and an appropriate image of civic-minded dignity. This was typically expressed with imposing colonnades, pediments, and marble sculpture.

The 19th-century cultural enlightenment fostered an especially great age for Cuban theater architecture. Considered by the ancient Greeks to be the most important public building after the temple, the theater was closely identified with classical civilization and thus the ideal embodiment for Cuba's high cultural profile—both aspired to and achieved. The Marqués de la Torre built the first formal theater in

Designed by an Italian architect, Daniel Dall'Aglio, the 1863 Sauto in Matanzas was the model for most 19th-century Cuban theaters. While the upper story has a classical design complete with pediment, the ground floor incorporates a Cuban *portal,* into which carriages could drive (below). The caned cast-iron seats (left) were manufactured in the United States.

Many touring stars, including Anna Paplova, performed on the Sauto *stage (right),* which could be raised and lowered mechanically. A basement mechanical system leveled the main floor to allow dancing when the orchestra seats were removed for balls. Painted allegorical figures adorn the dome of the Teatro Caridad *(above),* funded by Marta Abreu de Estevez in 1884 "for the poor of Santa Clara."

Havana in 1767; Santiago's French community soon followed suit, albeit with a less imposing thatch-roofed structure. By the 1700s, it was also customary to stage performances in a city's main plaza, sometimes in a temporary "casa" built for this purpose. In the early 1800s, theatrical presentations took place in private *palacios* as well.

Inspired by French prototypes, the grand classical theaters of the 19th century offered a suitable setting for European touring companies—ranging from classical ballet to Italian opera—hosted by Cuban cities. Designed by an Italian architect, Daniele Dall'Aglio, the 1863 *Teatro Sauto* in Matanzas was the most impressive theater outside of Havana. It represented an important and prestigious project for the city, which raised funds for the design and construction by selling subscriptions.

The design, subject to strict specifications and decided by competition, incorporated an elegant five-story structure with a drive-in *portal* for coaches. The interior followed the basic scheme that had been inspired by the European

passion for opera, which had established a separate curtained stage and large auditorium with seats segregated by social class. A triple-tiered scheme of circular balconies (fitted with cast-iron seats purchased from the United States) and separate smoking salons was crowned with an elaborate neoclassical ceiling fresco. The *Sauto* set the standard for many sister theaters, including the *Milanés* in Pinar del Río and the *Tomás Terry* in Cienfuegos.

RELIGIOUS ARCHITECTURE

Cuban baroque church architecture found its full flowering in the second half of the 18th century when the tradition of richly carved and gilded interiors in the Churrigueresque style still flourished in many parish churches. Examples of such ornateness are the elaborate pulpit and *retablo* of 1766 *Parroquial Mayor* funded by the second countess of Casa Bayona in the small town of Santa María de Rosario outside of Havana. The style peaked in the vividly contoured facade of the Havana Cathedral, completed around 1777 and endowed as a cathedral in

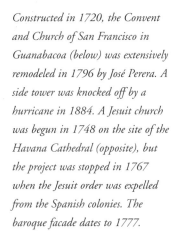

Constructed in 1720, the Convent and Church of San Francisco in Guanabacoa (below) was extensively remodeled in 1796 by José Perera. A side tower was knocked off by a hurricane in 1884. A Jesuit church was begun in 1748 on the site of the Havana Cathedral (opposite), but the project was stopped in 1767 when the Jesuit order was expelled from the Spanish colonies. The baroque facade dates to 1777.

The richly carved pulpit and altar of the 1766 Church of Santa María del Rosario in a small village founded by the Condes de Bayona make this the most sophisticated rural church interior in Cuba. Paintings are by José Nicolas de la Escalera, a noted artisan from the Canary Islands who also worked on the Convent of Santo Domingo.

1787. The facade design, distinguished by broken, serpentine planes of convex and concave curves dynamically opposed by angular broken cornices, derives from Francesco Borromini's 1667 *San Carlo alle Quattro Fontane* in Rome, and reflects a revival of Italian influences among the architects of Cádiz in this period.

During the 19th century, the increased secularization of the cultural laity and the rise of French-oriented rationalism and Freemasonry contributed to the declining power of Roman Catholicism and a corresponding separation of church and state. Freemasonry was becoming widespread. The Catholic Church was identified with the Spanish domain, and many Creole *independistas* joined the Freemasonry movement, which was a center of covert activity against the Spanish monarchy during the late-19th-century independence movement. These changes coincided with the rise of neoclassicism and the outright rejection of the exuberant, even vulgar, iconography of the baroque style. The newly fashionable neoclassical aesthetic offered a suitably chaste antidote and was also considered to be in good taste. At the end of the

1700s, a royal order actually prohibited the florid Churrigueresque-style altars, which were to be replaced with simple altars supported on unadorned classical columns of marble, or of wood painted in imitation of marble.

While new churches reflected the neoclassical influence, older churches were often remodeled in that style as well. In this spirit, the *Havana Cathedral* received a new classical interior around 1814, which included new plastered vaults constructed with layers of thin bricks. (Stone vaults, in fact, were not widely found in the Caribbean because the more sophisticated masonry was expensive and dangerous in earthquakes; it was not uncommon for builders to experiment with alternatives.)[2] Churches often gained sedate, classically inspired facades; *Espíritu Santo* in Havana, one of the city's oldest church buildings (founded as an *ermita* in 1638), was remodeled in this way around 1847. New neoclassical church facades broke completely from the former baroque massing, often combining a pedimented temple front with a central spire in a symmetrical composition reminiscent of the traditional Anglo-Saxon church.

By the mid-1800s, religious architecture had rejected the baroque taste. The Church of Espíritu Santo in Havana, (above) built as an ermita in 1638, was remodeled with a classical facade in 1847. Both San Pedro (top, right) and the Montserrat Chapel (right) in Matanzas owe a debt to Italian Renaissance architecture. (The chapel statues were added for a movie set.)

The Cathedral of San Carlos, the oldest church in Matanzas, dates to 1730 but was remodeled with neoclassical elements, including the pilasters, during the next century.

The 1850 Church of
San Salvador del
Mundo in Havana
has a central spire
reminiscent of the
Anglo-Saxon tradition.

CUBA: 400 YEARS OF ARCHITECTURAL HERITAGE

During the same period, the monumental cemetery became an important element in the urban landscape. The two earliest and greatest examples in Cuba were the *Cementerio de Cristóbal Colón* in Havana, and the *Cementerio Santa Ifigenia* in Santiago, the burial place of Cuba's revered heroes of the independence movement, Carlos Manuel de Céspedes and José Martí.[3]

Designed by a Galician architect, Calizto de Loira, and modified by Cuban architect Eugenio Rayneri, the Colón cemetery (1871–86), was built on some fifty hectares owned by the Roman Catholic Church in Vedado. It was the city's major urban architectonic expression of the era and a monumental work of art at once creative, symbolic, romantic, and spiritual. The design echoes the explicitly symmetrical cruci-

Designed as cities for the dead, the cemeteries of Santa Ifigenia *in Santiago (left) and* Colón *in Havana (below) represent the monumental tradition of the 19th century. Plots were segregated by class. Social, professional, and mutual societies (for immigrant groups) also built tombs for their members; the Colón Cemetery contains ninety such monuments.*

form plan of a Roman camp, with the four quadrants set on a distinct diagonal to the evenly paced grid of Vedado's residential blocks. Two broad, landscaped avenues meeting at a centrally located chapel set in a 90-meter-wide circular plaza intersect the cemetery. An overlay of smaller streets and circular plazas form secondary cruciforms in each quadrant, while a massively scaled Romanesque-Byzantine triumphal arch of locally quarried coral stone, symbolizing the conquest of love over death, marks the main entrance. Embellishing the arch is a marble sculpture, *The Theological Virtues*, carved by the renowned Cuban sculptor José Vilalta Saaverda.

Initially, both cemeteries were extremely exclusive—Colon was open only to Spanish loyalists and members of the Havana *cabildo*—and families competed to build the most elaborate tombs. Many of the elaborate Carrara marble monuments were shipped from Italy in pieces then finished by Italian or Cuban sculptors. Social position dictated the location and size of plots; thus, these necropolises were in effect cities within cities, where in death, as in life, class standing meant everything.

DOMESTIC ARCHITECTURE

Spanish-colonial domestic architecture peaked in the late 18th century in the grand *palacios* of Havana, and a few decades later in such sugar capitals as Matanzas, Sancti Spíritus, and Trinidad. In the last third of the 1700s, many of the early colonial *palacios* on Havana's old squares were remodeled and enlarged, typically by extending the second story forward over the plaza and adding an arched *portal* underneath. The use of the patio plan lasted well into the 19th century, particularly in the more conservative interior cities. One new development was the addition of a second, smaller transverse patio, or *traspatio,* to the rear of the first on the ground floor. This was usually overlooked by a second-floor dining room. By the third quarter of the 1700s, the distinctive colored *vitrales,* or colored glass windows, associated with Havana's colonial architecture were prevalent, lending color and vitality to house facades. The richest ornamental treatments, however, always centered on the grandiose baroque entrance doors, usually crafted by local artisans.

A close relationship between detail and spatial solutions existed in the town and plantation

The Palacio Brunet *fronting Trinidad's main square was built around 1740 and later enlarged with a second story. The house, unusually large for a provincial city, recalls the* palacios *of Havana and is typical of the townhouses owned by wealthy planters with sugar plantations in the nearby Valle de los Ingenios.*

Restored in 1996, the 18th-century Palacio Cantero in Trinidad is decorated throughout with murals; tiles of Italian marble pave the floors.

THE LATE COLONIAL ERA

Opening off the central patio, the kitchen of the Palacio Cantero in Trinidad is distinguished by a massive oven-and-chimney system built of plastered mamposteria.

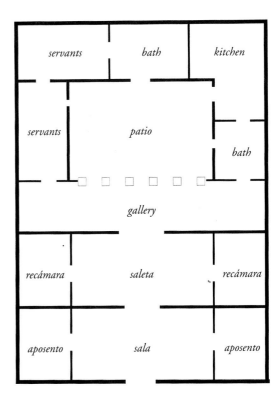

Late Colonial House

An 18th-century Creole palace (left)
rebuilt in 1846 shows the extremely high
sala ceiling characteristic of Sancti Spíritus,
once an affluent sugar capital. The exterior
of the house (below) was painted blue with
bands of trompe l'oeil marbleizing around
the windows.

The simple single-story house was the prevalent type in the provinces and usually shared walls with contiguous dwellings (right). The notable exception was the freestanding two-story Havana palace of the Creole aristocracy, exemplified by the late 18th-century Casa del Conde de Casa Lombillo (below).

By the 19th century, the ornamental designs of the crossbeams, or tirantes, *distinguishing the Mudéjar-inspired* alfarje *ceiling had become lighter and more open, while the proportions of the exterior portal (below) became more vertical.*

THE LATE COLONIAL ERA

Probably dating to the 1790s, this house is among the last of the baroque palaces built in Havana, and shows an elegant refinement of the stonework around the door. The ornate window lintels reflect the design of those on the Palacio de los Capitanes Generales.

Ionic pilasters on a house built for the Havana merchant Ricardo O'Farrill in the early 1800s mark it as one of the earliest in the city to display a classical influence.

houses of geographically and economically related areas, such as the city of Trinidad and the nearby Valle de los Ingenios, the center of the sugar mills in the area. The plantation house layout echoed the basic *sala* plan, although the two rear *recámaras* might serve as office and storeroom in this country version. The plantation *palacete* adopted the basic one-story *sala* plan prevalent outside of Havana but the house differed from city residences in that it was always freestanding, with the *portal* reinterpreted as a broad porch, designed to funnel breezes and provide extra living space.

The neoclassical style was first manifested in Havana, both in grand townhouses, such as the 1844 *Palacio de Domingo Aldama* (which combines a classical *portal* of Doric columns with a more traditional plan and colored-glass *mediopuntos* of the late-Baroque style), and in freestanding *quintas* (literally "one fifth," probably deriving from 1/5 hectare) starting to appear in Havana's El Cerro district and in city outskirts elsewhere in Cuba in the 1830s and 1840s. Recalling small Roman villas, they occupied spacious landscaped plots planted with park-like gardens much in the same manner as

Manuel José Carrerá, a Venezuelan-born architect, designed the Palacio de Domingo Aldama *in 1844. It was then the largest house in Havana and had one of the first water closets in the city.*

Fronted by a classical colonnade, the Casa del Conde de Santovenia *(left) was the quintessential summer villa, built in the 1840s in El Cerro. Set back from the street, the house was approached by a long drive and formal gardens. The* Villa Conchita *in Sancti Spíritus (below) also showed a graceful interpretation of classical elements.*

A mid-19th-century palace in Sancti Spíritus (right) reflects an ostentatious taste for the new classicism and a clear break with the Spanish baroque. The 1879 Palacio de la Marquesa de Villalba (below) by Eugenio Rayneri Sorrentino, aspired to be an Italian Renaissance Palace, but the architect still could not part with the portal at ground level.

An 18th-century Trinidad residence gained a new portico around the early 1800s; simple wood posts were crowned with wooden volutes to create Ionic columns.

the French *cafetales.* Inside, airy, marble-tiled rooms connected by arched *mediopuntos* flowed into one another, and were arranged around an open courtyard. Outside, a graceful columned peristyle encircled the house to complete the elegant effect; the pitch of the tiled roof was lowered and hidden behind a level parapet crowned at even intervals with classical urns.

The neoclassical influence continued to make its mark throughout the century. As with baroque elements, the neoclassical style was usually picked up with a somewhat indiscriminate application of individual parts—columns, a pediment, a classical urn—rather than through a cohesive understanding of the strict rules of proportion and composition inherent to ancient classical design. As a consequence, even in more sophisticated civic monuments the neoclassical was more a taste than an academic architecture, an effect aided by the widespread availability of mass-produced elements, such as cast-iron columns.

Old habits also hung on. A new neoclassical house might still retain the same plan used for the last two or three hundred years, but classical urns might appear on the roof, while a jigsawn wood column capital caught the curve, however distantly, of an Ionic volute. It was also common for early colonial houses to be updated with a new classically inspired porch.

TECHNOLOGY, MATERIAL, AND DECORATIVE TRADITION

As plantations proliferated and towns grew into cities almost overnight, a kind of boom-town building industry began to change the face of Cuba. Brickworks expanded; by the 1830s, there were some 700 in the colony, with more than half in the west. More remarkably, wood-frame construction also spread across the island. This was particularly true in Cuban towns with direct links to the U.S. Gulf Coast ports of Galveston, Mobile, and New Orleans, which exported quantities of Southern pine to the island.

Although the tradition of wood building dated to the earliest days of Cuba, the island's once-vast forests had been virtually obliterated by the land-consuming sugar *ingenios,* where wood was also used to fuel furnaces. The reappearance of wood was linked to new U.S. supplies of the material, and the introduction of the lightweight balloon-frame around the 1870s, which made use of milled lumber and mass-produced nails. There was also a growing market for mass-produced gingerbread trim and entirely prefabricated houses manufactured in North America. These could be ordered by catalog, shipped in numbered pieces to the island, then put up in a matter of days under the supervision of a local builder or engineer.

These simple prefab buildings with balloon frames and wood siding were used widely to

Mail-order gingerbread, possibly from the United States, embellishes a 19th-century balloon-frame house in Varadero.

Wood-frame houses on a slip of land known as Punta Gorda in Cienfuegos were prefabricated on the Gulf Coast of North America, then shipped to Cuba at the turn of the century.

Built in the mid-1800s, the first train station in Matanzas was a hipped-roof wooden structure (right), which now serves as a residence. The former fishing village on Cayo Smith (now Cayo Granma), an island in Santiago Bay, was a popular summer retreat earlier in the century (below).

The two-story veranda of balloon-frame houses on the Isle of Youth (above) and in the port city of Cienfuegos (left) recalls an element found elsewhere in the Caribbean and on the Gulf Coast of the United States. It rarely appears in Cuba outside of coastal settlements.

build modest housing in the plantation *bateyes,* spa towns, such as San Miguel de los Baños, and virtually all port cities. In his widely cited journal, the 19th-century traveler Baron de Humboldt remarked on the proliferation of "light and elegant" wooden houses around the Bay of Havana, from La Punta toward San Lázaro and La Cabaña toward Regla—all "ordered from the United States just as one would order furniture."

Mass-produced sheet metal (widely used for *batey* roofs) and molded cast iron were important products of Cuba's commercial and economic development as well. Cast iron was first used for railroad and *ingenio* construction, and widely used for warehouse construction in Havana, Matanzas, and Cárdenas. It was soon considered such an important material that it appeared as a subject of study at the *Escuela Pro-*

The Molokoff Market in Cárdenas is one of the only surviving cast-iron market structures in Cuba. Built at the turn of the century, it is designed with a cruciform plan, crowned with a dome, and occupies an entire block.

fesional as early as 1863. Belgian and U.S. manufacturers, including James Bogardus, who established a New York factory for cast-iron beams and columns in 1849, imported the material, but there were also Cuban makers.

Mass-produced in strong, interchangeable parts, the material proved highly economical for warehouses and industrial buildings, and was well suited to large-span structures like public markets. It was also adapted to circular stairs, slender lightweight columns, and the *guardacantones* (corner guards) marking the doorways of carriage entrances. Ornate, wrought-iron window grilles also began to replace the traditional wooden *rejas* by the turn of the century.

The new availability of materials more than satisfied the Cuban proclivity for color and embellishment. The initial use of colored glass *vitrales,* including both the *mediopuntos* and rectangular *lucetas* (transoms), dates to the last third of the 1700s. The arched profile of the *mediopunto* was especially adaptable to neoclassical design (although the garish colors were perhaps its antithesis). Although the glass was imported from the United States and Spain, the wood-framed *vitrales* were crafted on the island,

Decorative wrought-iron (left) and cast-iron (below) began to replace turned wood elements in the 19th century.

and the taste for their intense colors and patterns appears to have been a peculiarly Cuban phenomenon.

The original purpose of colored glass was to filter sunlight, and the windows appeared on facades of both public and residential building as well as around the interior courtyards. Partial-height double doors known as *mamparas* were also characteristic of 19th-century Cuban houses. Used to divide rooms without closing off the spaces completely, these, too, typically featured ornamental glass insets, decorated with cut-crystal patterns or delicate transfer designs, often in neoclassical floral patterns.

Fanlights known as mediopuntos were designed to light rooms that opened off the central enclosed patio. Louvered doors provide ventilation.

Ornamental tile also became an increasingly conspicuous addition to the Cuban house toward the turn of the 20th century. The popularity of colored concrete tile, called *mosaico hidráulico,* coincided with imports from Spanish manufacturers such as Escofet Tejera & Cia. in Barcelona, whose colorful patterns were reproduced widely throughout the Caribbean.[4] *Mosaico hidráulico* was particularly prevalent in borders and wainscot accents. *Azulejos,* enameled ceramic tiles made with oxides and glazes, were another fashionable innovation. This material was imported primarily from Seville.

The lobby design of the Hotel Globo *in Pinar del Río combines a fashionable pressed-tin wall covering, ceramic tiles, and a cast-iron newel post.*

Ceramic tiles with Moorish-inspired patterns (above) were shipped to Cuba by the thousands from Spanish manufacturers and incorporated into complicated wall patterns. The more durable colored concrete tile (right) was used for floors.

EXPRESSION WITH PAINT

Despite the impact of manufactured goods, the most significant decorative expression of the late colonial period remained decorative wall painting. This remarkable art traced a unique development in Cuba. To be sure, wall painting was practiced elsewhere in Latin America, but it was limited almost exclusively to church interiors in other colonies; didactic pictorial compositions depicted religious themes designed to underscore missionary teachings.

In Cuba, however, decorative painting was used widely for religious, civic, and domestic buildings alike. Even in the 1500s, the New Laws of the Indies dictated rich saturated colors for building facades, both to refresh the eye and

The Palacio Borrell *was built for a wealthy Catalonian family that settled in Trinidad and became successful planters. The* sala *was decorated in 1838 by an Italian artist from Florence who was commissioned to work on several residences in the city.*

Wall painting was typically used to create the effect of wainscoting, crowned with a patterned border, or cenefa *(right). Beasts and mythological figures were incorporated into the unusual painted decoration that distinguish* Guachinango *(below), a plantation house in the Valle de los Ingenios.*

cut the glare of the sun. The practice persisted into subsequent centuries, perhaps because the tints—shipped to Spain from South America—were inexpensive and widely available. The stone facades of the 18th-century baroque Havana cathedral and the government buildings on the *Plaza de Armas* of the same era were, in fact, originally painted in several colors.

By the second half of the 18th century, mural painting had become widespread outside of Havana, particularly in towns such as Sancti Spíritus and Trinidad, where the affluent planter class set the standards of taste. Used primarily in the formal *salas,* interior compositions emphasized painted *cenefas,* or wainscot-height bands that were often echoed with corner and window borders. Early motifs were simple geometric shapes worked in earth-toned pigments, but by the 19th century patterns evolved into classically inspired floral motifs in translucent blues, pinks, and greens. Many designs appear to have traveled to Cuba via the European salon culture and may reflect the contemporary excitement over wall paintings discovered in Pompeii and other ancient Roman cities.

It is not certain why this art was so fully developed in Cuba. One theory is that the decorative paintings served as a kind of heraldry for the Creole nobility, who often purchased their titles. In any case, the elaborate paintings were certainly an overt expression of wealth and class standing. At least some of the murals, done in mineral pigments on wet plaster, were the work of professional European fresco artists.

Recent restoration work reveals that mural painting was also remarkably prevalent on building exteriors. In addition to solid colors, walls were transformed with trompe l'oeil brushwork known as *falso despiezo,* which created the illusion of dressed stonework, often colored in blue or yellow and traced with white trompe l'oeil mortar joints. Intricate floral motifs and trompe l'oeil marbleizing were common as well. During the late 19th-century independence movement, architectural painting acquired political significance. Facades bearing a color scheme in red and yellow (the hues of the royal standard) signaled the sentiments of Spanish loyalists. *Independistas* painted their houses blue and white, the primary colors of the blue, white, and red Cuban flag, which would finally fly over the new republic in 1902.

Sancti Spíritus was a center for decorative painting, which began to feature classically inspired motifs by the 1800s (top). Many house exteriors in the town were painted in a trompe l'oeil masonry pattern known as falso despiezo *and had decorative cornice bands (above).*

Part IV

THE REPUBLICAN ERA

1898–1959

Completed in 1928, the classically inspired Cuban Capitolio *recalls the U.S. Capitol in design and reflects the spirit of the republican age. The stone-clad dome is supported by a steel frame and was intended to have stylized palm leaves that were never executed.*

Brief but turbulent, Cuba's republican era represents a complex balance of challenge, change, promise, and disappointment. By the late 1950s, Havana would be known as one of the most exciting, cosmopolitan cities in the world, but it had also become one of the more corrupt; the capital's glittering facade masked mounting inflation, deepening social divisions, and increasing disillusionment with a series of weak or self-serving political administrations—ending with the collapse of the Fulgencio Batista government on New Year's Eve, 1958.

Cuba began the twentieth century rebuilding from the independence wars, which had paralyzed the sugar economy and destroyed hundreds of *ingenios* and thousands of smaller farms, livestock ranches, tobacco *vegas,* or plantations, and *cafetales.* The Spanish-American war also finalized the disintegration of the social order that had shaped Cuban society for the last three centuries, leaving the dominating planter class, or the Creole bourgoisie, in economic ruin. As warehouses, equipment, and rail lines were destroyed, most mills shut down and few reopened after independence. The majority of planters were already carrying heavy mortgages and the high cost of capital made it impossible for most to re-finance their operations (only 7 of 70 ingenios survived in Pinar del Río, for example).[1]

The early 1900s brought a surge of immigrant laborers from the West Indies, the United States, and Europe, including some 200,000 Spaniards, a group that continued to dominate the island's mercantile sector. Although the Spanish-American war had left thousands starving and homeless, plans for new schools, hospitals, libraries, and public works programs were underway within a few years of the war's end. To help build them, the new *Escuela de Ingenieros, Electricistas y Arquitectos* was provisionally formed in 1900 at the University of Havana, then located in a former convent behind the *Plaza de Armas.* A central highway opened in 1931, followed a few years later by the island's first scheduled airline service.

Throughout this period, Cuba's economy remained bound to a one-crop sugar industry and fluctuated wildly. With the failure of the European sugar beet industry during World War I, Cuba once again became one of the world's primary sugar producers. But almost as soon as the "fat cows" had lined their ample pockets with gold during the famed 1920 "Dance of the Millions," (when sugar prices made an extraordinarily rapid three-month ascent, peaking at an unprecedented price of 22.5 cents per pound) the market crashed in 1921. A second crash came in 1929, followed by the Depression, then recovery in the mid-1930s. But even in prosperous periods, much of the profits flowed out of the country into the bank

The Cuban flag, first raised over the island in 1902, hangs over a balcony in the Santiago Cathedral.

accounts of absentee investors, including an increasing number of North Americans and Spaniards with interests in plantations, refineries, factories, and services, including railroads and telephone and electrical companies. Foreigners also dominated mining, tobacco, and the banking industry.[2] (Revolt against North American imperialism resulted in a second U.S. military occupation, from 1906-09.)

The United States, which had long recognized prime security interests in the Caribbean, also regarded Cuba as a potential lucrative commercial trade market. North American involvement in Cuba solidified with the temporary turnover of the island by Spain to the U.S. government under the terms of the 1898 Treaty of Paris at the end of the Spanish American War. The United States government supervised the transition of power, occupying the island until 1902, when Cuba was established as an independent republic. Troops evacuated that year, but under provisions of the 1903 Platt Amend-

ment to the new Cuban constitution, North America secured the right to intervene in Cuban affairs, maintain permanent naval bases on the island, and control the Cuban foreign debt.

By the early 1900s, several thousand U.S. citizens were formal residents of the island; upper-class Cubans, in turn, had ample financial interests in North America, where many of them were educated. Favorable tariffs made the United States the controlling market for Cuban sugar, forcing economic dependency.

Meanwhile, U.S. investment in Cuban sugar mills steadily rose; by 1913, it was reportedly close to $200 million. At the peak of the "Dance of the Millions," North American ownership, both in complete and joint ventures, reached an estimated 40%–50% (although the mills were largely Cuban in name). By the end of World War II, the United States controlled the refinery industry. By 1958, some 80% of Cuban imports, funneled almost entirely through Havana, came from the United States.

One of the most important outcomes of Cuba's changing economic ties was the development of a new middle class. The Creole aristocracy of the colonial period had more or less disappeared with the failure of the sugar mills between the Ten Years War (1868–78) and the last independence war. By the 1950s, not a single sugar plantation still belonged to the family of an original Spanish grantee.[3] No new upper class ever really replaced the old order. The haute bourgeoisie, comprising affluent businessmen and merchants, rather than an aristocracy of planters, essentially became the new upper class. This influential social group served as the primary liaison between international investors and the local Cuban market for raw goods while supporting a growing middle class of white-collar professionals necessary to the developing economy.

Together, the import-export economy, surging population growth, and the new bourgeois class underscored a widening division between the capital and the rest of the island. As Havana became the center of the Cuban universe, cities like Trinidad that were well off the central highway languished, while investment and development completely bypassed the countryside. State building programs primarily were limited to Havana and a few other cities considered a potential draw for tourist dollars. For the most part, they were directed to high-profile public

monuments, while many public works and road improvement projects benefitted from lucrative speculative development in which several presidential administrations had vested interest.

Speculation and tourism were in fact among the primary economic forces to shape 20th-century Cuba prior to the revolution. During the early years of the republic North American and Cuban land companies purchased vast property tracts (some covering 20,000 acres) and defunct estates from former plantation owners devastated by the war. As early as 1905, a reported 13,000 North Americans owned land in Cuba, worth more than $50 million, and title to about 60% of rural estate and farmland was also in the hands of North Americans or U.S. real estate development companies, with another 15% owned by Spaniards (thus putting Cuban ownership at only 25%).[4] Large tracts were developed with new sugar mills known as *centrales*. These included substantial factory-like production centers often located directly on private piers in a port rather than in the heart of the the cane fields. Demanding huge amounts of cane, the *centrales* required more land than the former *ingenios,* as well as the ownership of deepwater ports.[5]

To accommodate the expanding middle class, towns that had started spreading suburbs into their undeveloped fringes in the late-19th century continued to do so. As early as 1909, Santiago gained two planned residential developments

Reflecting North American models, the 1909 suburb of Vista Alegre in Santiago incorporated a broad central boulevard with a landscaped median; freestanding houses occupied large lots.

that made a marked break with the colonial fabric of the old city. The largest, Vista Alegre (Happy View), incorporated a grid of neat, square lots with a central landscaped boulevard. Like many Cuban suburbs, Havana's Vedado included, it accommodated a range of family incomes from middle to upper-middle class.

The first real fortunes in real-estate speculation were made at the start of World War I during the "dance of the millions" and were well-represented by the lavish single-family residences in eclectic, neoclassical, and revivalist styles going up in Vedado, Vista Alegre, and other Cuban suburbs. By this time, several Cuban-based architectural firms such as that of Rafecas y Toñarely, Albarrán y Bibal, Mata y Sánchez, Moenck y Quintana, Eugenio Rayneri y Cía, Morales y Mata, Govantes y Cabarrocas, Eugenio y Ernesto Batista, and Arellano y Mendoza were winning prestigious private commissions.

Well-known North American firms were working on a limited number of projects in Cuba by the 1920s and 1930s, among them Carrère and Hastings, McKim, Mead and White, Kenneth Murchison, Walker and Gillette, and Schultze and Weaver, who redesigned several existing buildings in Havana.

But architecture firms were not responsible for the majority of residential projects. Large private construction businesses, including U.S. companies like Purdy and Henderson (which supervised the Cuban Capitol project), began to control many building projects from start to end. Outside of the best neighborhoods, building in modest speculative developments was left to the lower-paid *maestro de obras* and bricklayer, working without an architect's design.

A second boom for the construction industry came after World War II, when a housing shortage fed another speculative frenzy. Mean-

The grand scale and ostentatious aspect of houses like the 1917 neo-Moorish Palacio del Valle *in Cienfuegos deliberately reflects the fortunes made by "fat cow" planters and merchants before the Depression.*

Radiating side streets south of Havana's Parque Central *frame narrow views of the Cuban National Capitol, which was deliberately designed to dominate vistas throughout Havana.*

Speculative construction during the first half of the 1900s resulted in the dense buildup of Central Havana.

CUBA: 400 YEARS OF ARCHITECTURAL HERITAGE

while, a sequence of urban development plans for Havana outlined ideas for a new civic center proposed for a range of areas of the city where landholders (counting numerous politicians) stood to make millions by selling off plots for public buildings and contiguous residential zones. A 1922 proposal by Enrique Montoulieu recommended placing the civic center in the undeveloped area around the *Quinta de los Molinos,* for example. In a similar vein, landowners with interests in the Havana coastline west of the Almendares River were influential in persuading Cuban president Gerardo Machado to commission a 1926 master enlargement plan for the capital. Actually signed into law the following year, this proposal was geared to lucrative tourism, business, and residential building deals based on extensive speculation, often in areas where illegal land divisions ignoring zoning codes were overlooked.

By the second half of the 1950s, about three-quarters of the investment in Cuban construction (more than $430 million) occurred in Havana. As the overcrowded center of the city could no longer support the population, dozens of new neighborhoods developed.

Important catalysts were the 1952 Law of Horizontal Property (*Ley de Propiedad Horizontal*), which encouraged investment in apartment projects by allowing the investors to amortize the cost over long-term payments, and the 1954 *Ley de Fomentos de Hipotecas Aseguradas* (FHA). This permitted developers to borrow on mortgages and made it economically feasible to build small single-family rental houses. Characterized by tiny lots averaging four meters across and thirty meters deep, these were so prolific that they were nicknamed FHA houses. By the end of the decade almost three-quarters of the houses in the capital were rentals.[6]

In the race to put up the most buildings in the shortest period of time, construction quality deteriorated in all but the best neighborhoods. Most notable among the more exclusive new suburbs with better housing were the western Havana developments, where the more upper-class districts of Miramar, Marianao, and Country Club (now Cubanacán) were built up after two Almendares River tunnels (1953 and 1959) connected these areas to downtown Havana. Country Club, the site of large residences and prestigious private clubs, is significant for

its parklike design of enormous lots and winding tree-lined streets founded in the garden-city tradition. By contrast to older districts like Vedado and Vista Alegre, naturalistic landscaping obscured the houses; secure in their wealth, affluent *Habaneros* no longer felt it quite so necessary to show it off, as was common in the boom years earlier in the century.

MASTER PLANS

Although several Cuban leaders and presidents attempted to reconfigure Havana's urban profile, no presidential administration surpassed the predilection to public display shared by Gerardo Machado (1925–33) and Fulgencio Batista (1940–44; 1952–58). Both men were responsible for commissioning the two most significant urban master plans of the era: Jean-Claude Nicolas Forestier's 1926 Beaux-Arts scheme and a modernist plan directed by José Luis Sert (1958).[7]

Although Machado's projects included government buildings for several provincial towns, the Model Prison on the Isle of Pines (now Isle of Youth), and the central highway, most of his ambitious program focused on the capital, to be redesigned under the most ambitious comprehensive plan since that of the colonial governor Miguel Tacón in the 1830s.

Machado and his Secretary of Public Works, Carlos Miguel de Céspedes, envisioned Havana as a model modern city that would rival any in Europe or North America. Their scheme included the Central Post Office (1929), an acropolis-like complex for the University of Havana, a lavish neoclassical capitol building, opulent hotels for Vedado, and the Forestier city-beautification plan. The budget was $50 million, to be raised by new gas, real estate and luxury taxes, and bonds issued by the Chase Manhattan Bank in New York.

Forestier was an internationally known landscape designer who had served as curator of Parks in Paris, designed gardens in Morocco and Spain, and created a park system for Buenos Aires in 1924. In creating the plan for Havana, he led an interdisciplinary team of professionals, including five young graduates from the École des Beaux-Arts. Among several Cuban architects and engineers in the group were Emilio Vasconcelos, I.I. del Alamo, Raúl Otero, Raúl Hermida, along with artists Manuel Vega

The Model Prison on the Isle of Youth (right and below) was built under president Gerardo Machado in the early 1930s. The complex of circular structures with rings of cells was based on the design of a penitentiary in Joliet, Illinois.

and Diego Guevara. Forestier's proposed designs for Havana paralleled many ideas for a comprehensive, socially aware city beautification program already being promoted by the Cuban architect Pedro Martínez Inclán, who advocated public art, parks, and land reserves as a means of providing a better urban experience for all classes. A belated manifestation of the City Beautiful movement, Forestier's own plan also took into account the social, natural, physical, *and* historic context of Havana. The scheme proposed to preserve the colonial district, while creating a new metropolitan center, conceived of as a gigantic park. Avenues of trees, landscaped malls, and parterres would define the city, enhanced by ensembles of civic buildings and an interplay of open and closed spaces. At the plan's heart were two broad, straight boulevards (east/west and north/south) set on a cross axis. These were meant to connect a new maritime/rail terminal on the harbor to the east and a future botanical garden to the south with a centrally located Plaza Cívica just south of Vedado, near the Quinta de los Molinos and the University. Here, a related complex of monumental cultural and government buildings, including a Museum of Flora, a Museum of Fauna, and a Ministry of Agriculture (symbolizing Cuba's natural splendors), would frame a plaza set on a series of terraces adapted to the hilly topography of the site. Radiating from the center were several diagonal avenues reminiscent of Baron Georges-Eugène Haussmann's plan for Paris.

The crash of 1929 and Machado's fall from power four years later left these plans unfulfilled. Among the completed components is the University of Havana's classically inspired tiered staircase (1927), conceived as a suitably formal gateway to this center of higher learning, relocated to its present site above central Havana in 1905. Forestier also completed a monumental esplanade for the Capitol building and remodeled 19th-century *Paseo del Prado* with a double aisle of laurel trees bordering a raised pedestrian mall running directly down the center of the boulevard. Cutting through flanking rows of grand columned houses, this majestic avenue formed an important north/south axis from the landscaped *Parque Central* (location of turn-of-the-century hotels, clubs, and, beyond the south end, the National Capitol) to the

Malecón. In doing so, it framed a tunnellike view of the *Castillo del Morro* across the bay, one of Havana's most familiar symbols of colonial history. Forestier's work also included remodeling the Malecón, the seaside roadway and promenade constructed from the north end of the Paseo del Prado to Lealtad in 1901 under the auspices of U.S. General Leonard Woods

One of the few completed elements of Jean-Claude Nicolas Forestier's 1926 master plan for Havana was the Paseo del Prado, *designed with Cuban architect Raúl Otero. The axial boulevard was planted with laurel trees to shade a median lined with benches of coral rock.*

In 1927, Jean-Claude Nicolas Forestier, Raúl Otero, and César Guerra collaborated on the eighty-eight-step entrance fronting the University of Havana (above); the secondary side stairs have a deliberately different rhythm. The seaside Malecón curves along the bay to Vedado (right), now dominated by the Hotel Nacional, *designed by the firm of McKim, Mead, and White.*

(1899–1902). Designed to incorporate a series of changing vistas and small, pleasant green areas, the avenue was extended west (eventually to the Almendares River) and southeast from the *Castillo de San Salvador de la Punta* to the wharves along the newly constructed *Avenida del Puerto.* This dramatic avenue, skirting the city at the edge of the sea, was the culmination of Forestier's vision for a cosmopolitan capital.[8]

Forestier's *Plaza Cívica* was not built, but the idea was later revived by Fulgencio Batista in collaboration with his Secretary of Public Works, Nicolas Arroyo. One of Batista's legacies to the city was the *Plaza de la República* (now *Plaza de la Revolución*), a direct descendent of the Forestier plan via two subsequent design competitions held in 1919 and 1940, during Batista's first administration. When the Plaza was completed in 1959 under Batista's second term, it combined ideas from the various designs. The *Plaza de la República* roughly occupied the proposed site near the *Quinta de los Molinos* suggested by Forestier and followed the concept of a broad, open plaza embraced by monumental public buildings. Instead of the museums, however, these included the Palace of Justice, National Library, and the modernist comptroller's office (*Tribunal de Cuentas*). At the center of the trapezoidal plaza, almost a kilometer in length, was the monument to José Martí, with a star-shaped base and statuary that combined elements from two earlier competitions.

The exuberantly playful Colony Hotel dates from a 1950s effort to bring foreign tourists to the Isle of Pines (now the Isle of Youth), which had been settled largely by North Americans earlier in the century. Hotel deigns of this period generally followed U.S. models.

CUBA: 400 YEARS OF ARCHITECTURAL HERITAGE

In 1955, Batista organized a National Planning Board (*Junta Nacional de Planificación*). The group was to promote a tourist plan that positioned Havana in a Caribbean triangle connecting it to Miami and the Yucatan Peninsula, targeting Vedado, the fishing town of Varadero, the Isle of Pines, and colonial Trinidad (near miles of unspoiled beaches) for development. The planning board also commissioned the Sert plan in 1958. Like the Forestier proposal, this was a team effort, involving Cuban architect Mario Romañach and other leading modernists, including Paul Lester Wiener and Paul Schultz. Although this tourist-oriented plan

Havana's Hotel Capri *typifies the high-rise establishments produced by Fulgencio Batista's tourism-development plan. The design was complete with a gambling casino and a rooftop pool.*

was never implemented, it is significant in its debt to the work of Le Corbusier, reflected in an extensive network of roads incorporating a series of Havana "superblocks" intersected by corridors of green. (These would have implications in the revolutionary era.) With total disregard for the historic center of the capital, it called for the demolition of the ground-floor facades of the colonial buildings in Old Havana to make room for covered pedestrian walkways. The plan ignored city topography and outlying districts, while blatantly emphasizing tourism. Although a planned artificial "pleasure island" built in the bay off the Malecón never materialized, Batista successfully developed tourist centers in Varadero and the Vedado section of Havana, where modern highrise hotels rivaled the Miami Beach skyline.

CIVIC BUILDINGS

As the first period of self-government in Cuba after four hundred years of colonialism, the republican era set a logical backdrop for a period of nationalistic civic monuments. While architectural activity concentrated in Havana, some administrations did fund civic, cultural, and social service projects in the interior.

Centrally located on the main plazas, republican-era civic buildings were typically a town's most prominent, and proudly reflected the full range of styles popular throughout the era. In the first decades of the century, the neoclassical canon—so closely associated with the civic pride and honor of ancient republics—remained a strong influence for such public monuments. This was in part due to the Beaux-Arts tradition favored for civic buildings by prominent North American firms whose work was widely published in current journals. Stylistic links to U.S. models were firmly established during both occupation periods in the early 1900s, first under U.S. General Leonard Woods, and later under the Director of Civil Construction, who was also North American. The tradition lasted until World War II. Built in the 1920s, the Santiago city hall, the current provincial *Poder Popular Municipal,* dominated by a pedimented temple front, and that city's *Museo Emilio Bacardí,* (a kind of reconfigured Parthenon with eclectic flourishes), are typical projects of the time.

The prime example of the monumental neoclassical mode, however, was the *Capitolio.* The final effort in a series of previously doomed

The imposing Matanzas Fire Station, completed in 1900, was among the country's first republican-era civic buildings and occupies a prominent place on the city's original plaza.

The 1899 Museo Bacardí *and a Santiago civic building now serving as the* Poder Popular Municipal *frame a downtown intersection with imposing classical facades.*

efforts, the Cuban National Capitol was begun in 1912 under president Mario Menocal (1912–20) on the site of a partially built presidential palace. Many architects, including Félix Cabarrocas, Mario Romañach, Eugenio Rayneri, Heitzler and Leveau (from Forestier's group), and Louis Betancourt, came and went (and sometimes returned) over the next years. The building was finally redesigned in 1928 during the Machado administration—but not before the first dome, part of the never-completed presidential palace, had been blown up with dynamite in 1918. Surprisingly cohesive after its many incarnations, the final design of the colossal, symmetrically massed structure measuring 692 feet long proved a grand statement of classical ceremony. Flanking colonnades of engaged Doric columns articulate the stone facade, which terminates in semicircular

pavilions at each end of the building. At the center, a tiered staircase approaches the 120-foot-wide entrance portico incorporating double rows of Ionic columns. Directly above rises the stone-clad dome, constructed with a steel frame (fabricated in the United States) and set on a drum circled by a peristyle in the Corinthian order. Rather than sitting in the exact center of the building, the dome rests forward near the front portico, accommodating a series of impressive public spaces on the first floor, including two large interior courts, a library, the *Salón Martí,* and the *Salón de los Pasos Perdidos,* embellished with marble paving, gold-leafed coffers, and a Statue of the Republic by the Italian sculptor Angelo Zanelli.[9]

Rayneri himself attributed the design of the *Capitolio* dome to the Parisian Pantheon. In addition to this French reference, the composition

Some 5,000 drawings were required for the design of the Cuban Capitol, which was built over a sixteen-year period. The approach was designed as a grand square with very little planting to detract from its formal aspect.

THE REPUBLICAN ERA

The main floor of the Capitolio incorporates two long lateral galleries leading from a central vestibule. The compass rose on the floor marks the location of the dome. Twenty-five percent of Machado's $50 million national budget reportedly was invested in this building, which has rich marble embellishments throughout.

CUBA: 400 YEARS OF ARCHITECTURAL HERITAGE

of the building as a whole recalls that of the U.S. National Capitol, in turn a descendent of the many early 20th-century U.S. State Capitols derivative of McKim, Mead and White's influential 1903 Rhode Island State Capitol in Providence. At the time of its completion, anti-imperialists criticized the building for its French and North American references. Nevertheless, the structure became one of the most familiar landmarks in Cuba and continues to dominate countless vistas throughout Havana.[10]

Havana's other prominent civic monument of the same period was the 1920 Presidential Palace (now the Museum of the Revolution) designed by Paul Belau and Carlos Maruri for a new site near the Malecón. This remains one of

With its domed grand staircase, the interior of the Presidential Palace reflects the grand tradition of a classical civic building.

Havana's most widely recognized eclectic buildings. Although the central pavilion front displays two-story arched windows flanked by Corinthian columns, the somewhat vague classical allusions give way to strong Spanish colonial overtones, most notably in the ground-floor *portales* and ornate towers, reminiscent of Spanish baroque church architecture. The interior appointments were done by the New York firm of Louis Comfort Tiffany.

By the 1940s and 1950s, Cuban civic buildings reflected the growing influence of modernism. The Palace of Justice (1952) in Santiago, for example, featured a squarely massed four-story design stripped of the orna-ment lavished on its predecessors—although the vertical supports in the front pavilion vaguely suggest columns. Begun the same year, the *Tribunal de Cuentas* (now Ministry of the Interior), designed for Batista's *Plaza de la República* in Havana by Aquiles Capablanca, was then highly acclaimed as an accomplished modernist design indebted to both Le Corbusier and Walter Gropius. Although the stark limestone building was devoid of historical references, it is notable for its incorporation of contemporary statuary and ceramic mosaics by Cuban artists, a reflection of the interest among the Cuban vanguard to celebrate Cuban artisanry.

The late art deco facade of *Palacio de Justicia in Santiago (left)* interprets the traditional classical portico with a modernist vocabulary. Many Santiago buildings were built in the art deco style after earthquakes damaged the city in the 1930s. The 1953 Ministry of Interior in Havana (below), by Aquiles Capablanca, shows the influence of Le Corbusier, but honors Cuban tradition in the use of local coralstone for the wall cladding. Added after the revolution, the facade sculpture represents Che Guevara.

The monument to José Martí in Havana's Plaza de la Revolución *was a collaborative effort built between 1938 and 1952. The 450-foot modernist obelisk dwarfs a more traditionally interpreted statue of the Cuban independence leader.*

CUBA: 400 YEARS OF ARCHITECTURAL HERITAGE

RELIGIOUS ARCHITECTURE

The Republican era brought about a dramatic change in the role of the Church in Cuba. The fight for independence had deepened the division between the Catholic Church, which supported the Spanish position, and Freemasonry, which had a strong base in the nationalist cause. Masonic ethos asserted the possibility of finding moral truth without religious intervention, and directly challenged the Church. Most independence leaders (José Martí included) were Masons, and Masonic lodges throughout the island had served as centers for anti-colonial activity.

Independence thus marked a victory for Masonic doctrine. One of the basic tenets of the 1901 Cuban constitution was the separation of Church and State, which was specifically designed to cut off government support for the Catholic Church and deprived it of tax rev-

enues. Religious teaching was banned in public schools and state subsidies for churches ended. This situation provided the right climate for the rise of Protestantism, which came to Cuba primarily from the United States and took a neutral non-political position.

Catholicism nevertheless remained the fundamental religion in Cuba, affiliated with the upper class and conservative press. But given the Church's reduced circumstances and the anti-Catholic political climate, new ecclesiastical building was not as significant in the republican period as in the colonial era. Since the first U.S. occupation, the Episcopal Church had an increasingly strong presence in Cuba and new Protestant commissions typically reflected Cuba-U.S. connections. In 1905, Bertram Goodhue, the first well-known North American architect to design a building on the island, was hired to create an Episcopal cathedral in Havana. The

Havana's Teatro Nacional *was designed in 1958 by the firm of Arroyo y Menéndez. It was one of the last Cuban civic buildings completed before the revolution.*

commission probably came through his friend James Gillespie, a North American who owned a house in Cuba; Goodhue had designed a house for Gillespie in California a few years earlier.[11]

Bertram Goodhue was already a respected church designer at home and his pavilions for the 1916 California-Pacific Exposition in San Diego would give impetus to a Spanish colonial revival movement in North America for the next two decades. His design for the *Santísima Trinidad Episcopal Cathedral* in Havana (no longer extant), was one of the very earliest examples of the style on the island and featured an elaborate Churrigueresque-style entrance that would be echoed in later buildings, including non-religious struc-

The Santiago Cathedral is the fourth on its site. The building was damaged by an earthquake in 1852 and reconstructed with a neoclassical façade in 1922. It fronts the Parque Céspedes, *the most important plaza in the city.*

tures such as the Cuban Telephone Building (1927, Morales y Cía.), in Havana.

Well into the century, new Catholic churches typically relied on Spanish revivalist designs, as exemplified by *La Iglesia de Nuestra Señora del Carmen* (1927) designed by Félix Cabarrocas in Havana, and the basilica of the *Virgen de la Caridad del Cobre* near Santiago

(1927), the shrine to the island's patron saint.

After World War II, Protestant and Catholic congregations in new middle and upper-middle class suburbs commissioned new buildings in the current styles. *La Iglesia de San Antonio de Padua* and *La Iglesia de Jesus,* both in Havana's Miramar district, represent up-to-date modernist designs of the 1950s.

The Church of Santo Angel Custodio in Havana was largely destroyed by a hurricane in 1844; gothic spires were added when the church was redesigned between 1866 and 1871.

Although the Church of La Merced in Havana was begun in 1755, all of the current interior appointments, including the romantic dome paintings, were added during a remodeling in 1904 to reflect early republican-era sensibilities.

CUBA: 400 YEARS OF ARCHITECTURAL HERITAGE

The Spanish revival style basilica at El Cobre was built in 1927 to house the shrine of the Virgin of la Caridad del Cobre, special guardian of the Sierra Maestra. The three-bay facade and towers recall Cuba's Spanish baroque churches of the 18th century.

THE REPUBLICAN ERA

Designed by Eloy Norman and Salvador Figueras, the 1951 Church of San Antonio de Padua (above and right) is located in the Havana suburb of Miramar, which was developed after World War II. Elongated arches on the modernist facade could be distant references to the Cuban portal.

CUBA: 400 YEARS OF ARCHITECTURAL HERITAGE

SCHOOLS AND HOSPITALS

In the early years of the new republic, educational and health-care reform were among the primary initiatives for a modern Cuba. For the first time, the new constitution provided for a free, secular, and compulsory education. Some three thousand schools were established under the provisional U.S. government; most of these public schools, however, occupied existing buildings scattered throughout the countryside that had been vacated during the war. Private schools built with private funds were erected in most cities, and Catholic schools were prevalent as well. Most new rural schools were modest bungalows, but some more monumental structures were built in major cities. These generally followed the classical lines of the island's early civic buildings. A notable example is the *Instituto de Enseñanza Superior* in Havana. This impressive structure, designed to dominate a new area of development near the demolished city walls, features a columned pavillion front; it was designed in 1918 by Benjamín de la Vega at the behest of José Ramón Villalón, Minister of Public Works for president Mario Menocal.[12]

Aside from the University of Oriente in Santiago, higher education centered in Havana. The Catholic University of Villanueva was founded there in the 1940s to offer an alternative to the secular and more popular University of Havana. The University of Havana was the first university in the Spanish Caribbean region to be conceived as a whole, and its formal, axial composition of elongated blocks, typical of turn-of-the-century Beaux-Arts design, may owe something to Charles McKim's original 1894 plan for the campus of Columbia University in New York.[13] The setting atop a rocky promontory commanding spectacular views of central and old Havana and the bay behind symbolizes the classical concept that culture sits above society. The university's design and construction (1905–1940) brought together a team of prominent Cuban architects, including Enrique Martínez, Benjamin de la Vega, Joaquín Weiss y Sánchez, José Cárdenas, and Pedro Martínez Inclán.

The Cuban health-care system during this same period comprised large hospitals that were concentrated in the capital, as well as a network of *clínicas mutualistas,* which offered medical services at reasonable fees. Early 19th-century hospital and clinic architecture frequently incorporated independent pavilions, a principal borrowed from the Havana municipal hospital, which had been remodelled in 1886 following English and North American prototypes. The hospital structures were set around open plazas and an elaborate entrance arch took the place of a single dominant facade.[14] The Havana hospitals dominated the city center, Vedado, and the western suburbs. Marianao was the site of three prominent early modernist designs: the *Hospital de Maternidad Obrera* (1939) by Emilio de Soto, the *Sanitorio Infantil de la Habana* (1944) by Luis Dauval—an elongated boat-like design with stepback facade and curvilinear end pavilions—and the *Hospital Militar* (1940) by José Pérez Benitoa.

The secondary school in Nueva Gerona was one of many educational institutions dating from an early republican-era effort to build schools throughout the country.

The 1937 University of Havana library by Joaquín Weiss combines a strong sense of classical monumentality with art deco references, most notable in the Mayan-inspired column capitals.

CUBA: 400 YEARS OF ARCHITECTURAL HERITAGE

The Hospital Infantil Docente Pedro Borras *(top, left) in Havana and
the 1944* Sanatorio Infantil de la Habara Angel A. Aballi *in Vedado,
by Luis Dauval (top, right), are among the best examples of art deco
hospital architecture in Cuba. The* Los Angeles Hospital *in Santiago is
representative of traditional republican-era design.*

PRIVATE CLUBS

The growing focus on leisure, money, and social climbing spawned a new era of club architecture. One important inheritance from the 19th-century cultural renaissance was the *casino*. This social and cultural club continued to flourish throughout the island, typically housed in a substantial structure on the main plaza, as exemplified by the eclectic 1927 design in Sancti Spíritus. The two-story structure, now a public library, features a bowed pavilion front incorporating an arched portal and a columned balcony on the second floor.

A number of Spanish clubs also served as social and political centers for the regional societies of Galicians, Basques, Andalusians, and Catalonians residing in Cuba. These housed theaters, lecture halls, ballrooms, and gyms. The most notable examples were in Havana: the *Centro Asturiano* and *Centro Gallego* on the *Parque Central,* and the American Club and the *Casino Español* on the nearby *Paseo del Prado.*

Spanish social-club architecture expressed the allegiance of the patrons, primarily prosperous merchants, through strong, if eccentric, Spanish Revival overtones. Fronting the park, the *Centro Gallego,* for example, offers an ornate and startling counterpart to its sedate neighbor, the classical *Capitolio* (both buildings were built by the same North American construction company, Purdy and Henderson). Designed by the Austrian architect Paul Belau, the extremely eclectic and individualistic design of the *Centro Gallego* shows its Spanish colors in the use of ground-floor *portales,* tiered corner cupolas (reminiscent of the Geralda tower of the Cathedral of Seville), and a baroque cornice line. The curving transom mullions and use of colored glass echo the baroque window treatments of

The former Casa de Fausto Menocal, *designed by Emilio de Soto in 1921, features a grand ballroom that now serves as the site of Cuban wedding ceremonies.*

Havana's colonial monuments, such as those of the *Palacio del Segundo Cabo*. The *Centro Gallego* was actually an ambitious renovation project of the former 19th-century Tacón Theater, which was absorbed into Belau's new design. One of the two ornate entrances that dominates the facade leads to the theater (still in use); the other offered access to such club facilities as libraries, and smoking, billiard, and dining rooms for the members.

Complete with grand staircases, domed and coved ceilings, and marble floors, such interiors paralleled the ostentation of the exteriors with overscaled staircases, elaborate marble detailing, and appointments designed as constant, visual reminders of the patrons' wealth and Spanish heritage. As was usual in the Cuban Spanish revival style, historical references were liberally mixed. The exterior of the 1927 *Centro Asturiano* (which also incorporated an old theater), for instance, features playful stone ornament in the spirit of the Cuban baroque, while some of the original club furnishings were based on pieces from *El Escorial*, the famed 16th-century monastic palace built near Madrid during the reign of Philip II.

The Casino Español *in Matanzas exemplifies early 20th-century social-club architecture with its ostentatious massing and ornate facade ornament.*

The Centro Asturiano in Havana was built from the winning design of a 1918 competition by Manuel del Busto, a Spanish architect form Gijón. The building committee had stipulated that the design "conform to the purist classicism of the Spanish Renaissance style."

One of the most important
Spanish social clubs in Cuba was
the Centro Gallego, *which was
designed by Paul Belau and
incorporates the old* Teatro
Tacón. *The elaborate facade
decoration suited the flamboyant
tastes of the members, prosperous
families of the Cuban merchant
class. A performance of* Aïda
*marked the inauguration of the
club in 1915.*

Private sports, beach, and country clubs also proliferated during the republican era. Most notable examples were in Havana, among them the 1912 Vedado Tennis Club, the Lyceum Lawn Tennis Club, and a host of others scattered up the western beaches after a bridge was built over the Almendares River, including the 1924 Havana Yacht Club, designed by José Alejo Sánchez and Rafael Goyeneche, a Mexican architect with strong roots in Cuba. By contrast to the Spanish social clubs, institutions such as the yacht club were usually the domain of old and established Cuban families, and usually expressed a conservative sense of tradition with elegant and controlled designs in a North American Beaux-Arts mode. One of the great examples was the *Gran Casino Nacional*, redesigned from an older building in 1928 by Lloyd Morgan, a partner in the American firm of Schultze and Weaver. Morgan's severely symmetrical two-story composition featured a monumental central pavillion front with a grand porte-cochere conceived as a triumphal arch and suitably ornamented with stone panels cast with a procession of classical figures.

As with other types of buildings, club designs began to reflect up-to-date modernist trends after World War II. One of the last clubs built before the revolution was the ultramodern *Club Náutico* by Max Borges, Jr., a futuristic composition of arched concrete shells and sweeping roof meant to recall ocean waves.

The grand main staircase of the Centro Gallego is typical of the interior public spaces of Havana social clubs designed to compete with other clubs serving members of Cuba's aristocratic class.

The sedate Beaux-Arts facade of the Havana Yacht Club (above) reflects the conservative taste of the members, primarily patrician Creoles. The oldest private club in Cuba, it was founded in 1888; the Miramar clubhouse was designed in 1924 by Rafael Goyeneche and José Alejo Sánchez. The 1957 Club Náutico, a Miramar swimming club (right), featured a fashionable modernist design by Max Borges, Jr. Shell vaults of reinforced concrete linked various separate structures.

MOVIE HOUSES
AND NIGHTCLUBS

By the 1930s, Hollywood culture had saturated Cuba. (Hollywood, in fact, maintained movie studios in Miami.) Havana movie houses now featured first-run North American films. The heyday of the movie theater coincided with the early modernist art deco and moderne styles, which proved ideally suited to this type of commercial architecture. Offering a startling contrast to the traditional backdrop of Cuban cities, the streamlined, futuristic facades tempted ticket-buyers with a sense of fantasy and magic that continued inside the building. Even today, the 1938 *Cine-Teatro Fausto* dominates Havana's *Paseo del Prado;* the distinctive facade, which depends on a striking interplay of vertical and horizontal ribs, might have been transplanted from Miami Beach's Ocean Drive.

The Cine Oriente *in Santiago (above) and the 1936* Cine-Teatro Fausto *in Havana (left), by Saturnino Parajón, show a similar approach to art deco movie palace design in their pastel coloring and simplified vertical facade elements.*

The Cinema Arenal *in Miramar makes a playful reference to the baroque church facades of earlier centuries.*

One of the great moderne style theater interiors dating from this period is that of the *Edificio America* (1941), where tiers of curvilinear box seats melt into the walls of the vaulted auditorium. The terrazzo floor of the lobby includes an inlaid map of the world with the island of Cuba—the center of the world, of course—triumphantly picked out in polished brass.

Nightclubs were another product of the Cuban tourist industry. Although most were best-known for sizzling dance routines, the famed 1951 *Cabaret Tropicana* is one of the most imaginatively conceived modernist commercial buildings in Havana. Here, as in his *Club Náutico,* Max Borges, Jr., explored the use of thin-shell concrete vaults. Ranging in span from forty to ninety feet, five arches framed two circular dance floors and orchestra stages, while curving bands of clear glass filled the spaces in between. The entire front of the tallest vault was also glass-glazed, with sliding doors across the base. The idea was to provide a continual shift in views both outdoors and in as dancers moved around the main room, which has since been altered.

The 1941 Cine América in Havana (above) was one of two theaters incorporated in a design by Fernando Martínez Campos and Pascual de Rojas that also included an apartment tower. A superb example of the streamlined moderne style, a late phase of the art deco, the movie house featured cantilevered boxes offering an unobstructed view of the screen. The 1954 Cabaret Tropicana (left), by Max Borges, Jr., was designed with laminated thin-shell vaults and large expanses of glass intended to frame views of tropical foliage, which was brilliantly lit at night.

DOMESTIC ARCHITECTURE

The republican era opened with a severe housing problem. The Spanish-American war had left thousands of people homeless. Moreover, the classic pattern of the colonial period continued: As the middle and upper-middle class population supported new suburban development, deteriorated city centers became more densely populated with the lower classes. In urban areas, families crowded into rental properties known as *solares* or *ciudadelas.* These tenement-like structures housed dozens of people in one- or two-room quarters surrounding a courtyard containing communal cooking and laundry areas reached from the street by a narrow alley. Colonial *palacios* continued to be subdivided with loft-like *barbacoas,* or platforms that took advantage of the high ceilings. These old buildings were known as *cuarterias.* Shanty towns proliferated on city edges, while the majority of the rural populace continued to live in dirt-floor *bohíos,* most lacking electricity and plumbing.

Virtually all new domestic building, however, focused on speculative suburban development for the middle class and above. At the upper end of the income scale, suburbs offered precisely what the inner cities could not: space and greenery. It was no longer fashionable to live downtown. In Havana, the last of the urban palaces—their contiguous facades linked by long rows of *portales*—had been built in the city center by the end of the 1800s.

The now popular concept of the freestanding house in a landscaped garden found its first full flowering in the era of the "fat cows" before the crash of 1929. Early examples combined the concept of the freestanding house—introduced in the 19th-century *quintas*—with the eclectically conceived facade designs that had become fashionable by the turn of the century. In the teens and 1920s, these became increasingly gaudy in an era when displaying personal wealth was of tantamount importance to the new bourgeoisie.

One prevalent house type was a variation on the picturesque villa, asymmetrically massed with towers, bay windows, and porches breaking out of the former patio plan and detailed with decorative elements picked out from a hybrid of historical styles. On the first floor, the front *salas* (resembling the North American par-

The residence of Manuel Carvajal and Margarita Mendoza, Marqueses de Avilés, was commissioned in 1915 from Thomas Hastings of the New York architectural firm, Carrère and Hastings. The restrained Beaux-Art design, which originally included Pompeiian frescoes, was a sedate counterpart to the typically ornate domestic architecture favored during this period.

lor), a dining room, and perhaps a library or music room opened off a long hall and a grand staircase led to second-floor bedrooms, reflecting the trend toward rooms with very specialized uses. Among the notable changes was the improvement in plumbing, which made the bathroom, emblem of republican advancement, an inherent part of the plan and gave it a prominent place as a connector between bedrooms.[16]

Not all new houses were freestanding. Speculative rows fronted densely built streets in new urban developments, as well. Frequently, these were two-story multifamily houses in which the uniformly designed entry incorporated two doors: one opened to the ground floor and one led to a narrow stair approaching a separate dwelling above. In this way, each residence had a direct connection to the street.

In the first decades of the 1900s, gaudy embellishments in stucco and concrete began to replace more formal ornament carved in stone. This eclectic-style residence, with its tower recalling that of a Tuscan villa, typifies the residences built in that suburb until the 1930s, where most of Havana's upper class was then living.

French and North American glassmakers, including the New York firm of Louis Comfort Tiffany, were commissioned to design elaborate stained-glass appointments for Havana mansions. The reception room of the Villa Lita *in Vedado* exemplifies early republican-era taste in interior design.

Widespread speculation
during the republican
era resulted in houses of
a broad range of quality
and styles. Eclecticism,
represented by these
Pinar del Río residences,
was favored well into
the early 1900s.

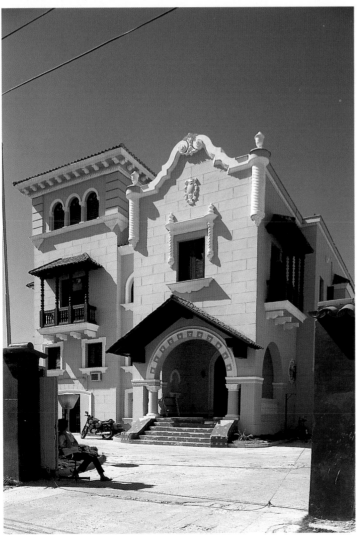

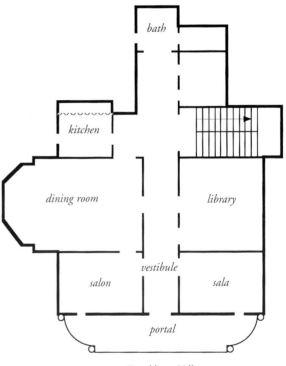

Republican Villa

Another whimsical eclectic
design distinguished a
Miramar villa, with the
asymmetrical massing
characteristic of early
republican-era houses.

THE REPUBLICAN ERA

As the century progressed, moderate-income neighborhoods were built up with small bungalows, modest "chalets" (one- or two-story houses without a courtyard), and variations on the basic one-story plan with an attached car port. By the 1940s, U.S. builders had introduced the modestly-priced stucco-faced cement-block "California" house to Cuban suburbs as well. This small-scale variation on the ranch house, with a single-story open plan, could be built from standard-issue plans.

In the same period, however, many of the most recognized modernist architects working in Cuba, including Rafael de Cárdenas (prolific designer of luxury houses in Miramar), Eugenio Batista, Mario Romañach, Frank Martínez, and Max Borges, Jr., were also exploring sophisticated suburban designs based on new themes of function, volume, light, freeflowing space, the integration of tropical greenery, and the creative use of mass-produced materials—including plywood and concrete. One of the most highly

By 1958, between one-third and one-half of Cuban houses had been built after World War II. A small Spanish-style villa in Guanabacoa (right) and a "California House" in the Vista Alegre suburb of Santiago (below) are examples of popular middle-class house styles.

An art deco style ziggurat profile accentuates the entrance to a simple wood-frame shotgun house in Santiago (left). The long narrow house type, one-room wide, is thought to have originated in Haiti and may have come to Santiago via sugar planters from that island. A modest residence shows the art deco style also influenced houses in Baracoa (below).

acclaimed is Romañach's 1948 house for Julia Cueto de Noval, a three-story rationalist work located in the Havana suburb of Country Club. This starkly rectilinear composition recalls the work of Richard Neutra, who made his own mark in Havana a few years later with his 1956 Alfred de Schultess house, a horizontally massed design with cantilevered beams and interior stone veneers. This house was commissioned as a winter residence by a cosmopolitan Swiss couple and is one of the only known residential works by an internationally known modernist in Cuba. Cuban architects Raúl Alvarez and Henry Gutierrez participated in the design and the gardens were by the Brazilian landscape architect Roberto Burle Marx.

Apartment-building design never reached the same level of sophistication as the single-family house. In the hands of local land speculators, the Cuban apartment house became the tool of building codes geared to exploiting a parcel of expensive land for maximum profit, spurred by the 1952 Law of Horizontal Property.

The concentration of the construction industry in the capital (and the threat of earthquakes elsewhere on the island) limited major apartment projects to Havana. Apartment houses typically followed the general stylistic lead of other buildings. During the early 1900s, art nouveau style rental blocks appeared in Central Havana; in the 1930s low-rise walk-up

Even in the modernist period, bright color remained important to Cuban design, as shown by a balcony in the Miramar section of Havana (above). The Casa de Julia Cueto de Noval *in the Country Club (now Cubanacán) section of Havana (right) was designed by leading Cuban modernists Mario Romañach and Silverio Bosch in 1948. Integrating light and tropical foliage was a constant theme of Cuban rationalist design.*

Fernando Salinas and Raúl González Romero used fluid poured-concrete forms in their 1950s Casa del Puente *(left), a Havana residence with overtones of modern Scandinavian design. The 1957* Casa de Rufino Alvarez *(below) was designed by Mario Romañach, who frequently experimented with wood screening and concrete veneers to create a play of light and shade.*

buildings in the art deco style proliferated in Miramar and other suburbs.

Among the city's first luxury apartment houses of note was the *López Serrano* in Vedado. When designed in 1932 by the Cuban firm of Mira y Rosich, the apartment block was the tallest building in Cuba even though its central tower—reminiscent of New York's Empire State Building—counted only fourteen stories. The symmetrically massed setbacks, vertical terra-cotta ribbing, and small but distinguished lobby—complete with ziggurat-shaped mirror inlaid terrazzo floor—call to mind similar art deco designs of the same period in Miami Beach, New York, and Los Angeles. The minimalist highrise designs of the post-War era are perhaps epitomized by the gigantic 1956 *Edificio FOCSA*, also in Vedado. This thirty-five story complex, hailed by its builders for its progressive approach to urban living, was conceived as

The Austrian-born architect Richard Neutra collaborated with the Cuban firm of Alvarez y Gutiérrez on the Casa de Alfred de Schultess *(right). The rationalist concrete-and-glass design, completed in 1958, stresses clarity of form and function. Combining community services with 400 individual family apartments, the 1956* Edificio FOCSA *(below) is loosely based on a Corbusian model, but failed to incorporate green spaces.*

The 1932 art deco style López Serrano apartment building in Vedado was among the first large investment projects erected after the 1929 Crash. The vertical shafts and tower setback show the clear influence of New York skyscraper architecture. The design, which comprises eight apartments per floor, is by Ricardo Mira and Miguel Rosich.

As the population increased and neighborhoods grew more crowded, land prices skyrocketed in the capital. Massive middle- and upper-middle class apartment buildings became one of the only viable investments for builders. Exploiting the possibilities of poured concrete, the undulating mass of the Solymar apartments by Manuel Copado dominated the Central Havana skyline when built in 1944 and continues to do so today.

CUBA: 400 YEARS OF ARCHITECTURAL HERITAGE

a self-contained city within a city: in addition to 400 apartments and a garage for even more cars, it boasted its own power plant, school, and a restaurant (called *La Torre*), on the twenty-eighth floor. Such amenities were perhaps the ultimate manifestation of a trend to luxury that would be cut short by the 1959 revolution just three years later.

Smaller apartment buildings ranging from four to six stories began to serve the growing middle class from the 1930s onward. Light shafts and inset balconies in this art deco Havana example (left) broke up the massing and increased natural ventilation. Completed just before the revolution, the 1959 Edificio del Seguro Médico (below) employed the narrow slab configuration then emerging in North American urban architecture.

Part V

THE REVOLUTIONARY ERA

1959–Present

The Fidel Castro-led revolutionary takeover of the Cuban government on January 1, 1959, marked a dramatic victory for an opposition movement built on growing disillusionment with pro-U.S. policy and intensifying social and geographical inequities. By the end of the decade, the political implications of the growing anti-Batista movement and the related economic uncertainty of the erratic import-export economy had thrown the middle class into a crisis. Always weak, the Creole industrial sector remained undeveloped and the sugar industry was unable to sustain growth. Outside of sugar, more than one half of the national industrial production was centered in Havana. Cubans on average enjoyed one of the highest standards of material living in Latin America, second only to that of Venezuela. However, measured against the U.S. economy on which the Cuban living standard depended, the numbers appeared in a different light: Cuba's $375 average per capita income ranked even lower than that of the poorest U.S. state, Mississippi.[1]

Havana's social, economic, and physical isolation from the rest of the island was symbolic of the currents of polarization running through every aspect of Cuban life. An estimated one-fifth of the island's population of about 6.5 million—along with the majority of wealth and services—was concentrated in the capital, six times larger than the second-largest city, Santiago. With many millions of dollars invested in Cuba, the United States controlled 40% of the sugar industry spread among about 150 *centrales* dispersed throughout the country.

Havana and the western provinces fared best. The standard of living was markedly worse in the countryside, particularly in Oriente. In general, the rural peasant population had little access to education or health services because country-wide building programs for such facilities had been sporadic and limited since the 1930s. The majority of rural families lived in dirt-floored *bohios,* most without electricity and plumbing. A good one-third of all urban housing was also substandard. The urban fringes of Cuban cities melted into vast cardboard slums; prostitution, illegal gambling, and drug trafficking were rampant in Havana. Public works programs throughout the country had come to a standstill as building projects focused on residential speculation.

Based on Marxist-Leninist ideology, Castro's reforms were swift. With the aim of rebalancing the urban-rural equation, the focus shifted pointedly away from Havana and turned to developing agro-industrial production in the countryside, and to improving standards of education, health care, and housing for all Cubans. In an effort to nationalize industry and the banking system, the state confiscated most foreign- and many Cuban-owned proper-

ties and formed a Ministry of Exterior Commerce to control imports and exports. Two new agrarian reform laws (1959 and 1963) nationalized large plantations and put the majority of Cuban farmland under state control, limiting farm size and authorizing the formation of state-run cooperatives and collectives.

A parallel set of real estate regulations outlawed speculation and the mortgaging of empty lots. Under the 1960 Urban Reform Law, all existing leases and mortgages were cancelled, and rents reduced to 10% of a tenant's income. This effectively choked off the rental revenues that had been a primary source of investment for the Cuban middle class, principally through income gained from new rental construction or through lending financing for the same against mortgage security. Thousands of families who had all their savings in real estate lost everything. Under the new laws, rent was payable to the state, but tenants were responsible for all upkeep costs. Rent payments could be amortized toward the nontransferable purchase of a house, but this policy largely failed to put buildings into private hands because purchase was contingent on prompt payments. In the early chaotic months of the revolution, thousands of tenants did not keep up with rent payments because landlords did not collect regularly, courts did not evict[2], and occupants were reluctant to sign agreements authorizing title to property confiscated by the State. Thus, despite efforts to the contrary, ownership of a majority of former private property landed in state hands and the government became a landlord despite its initial intent not to do so.[2]

Relations between all denominations of the Church and the Castro government shifted frequently during the first decade of the revolutionary era. The theoretical emphasis of Marxist-Leninist ideology is on atheism, and by the early 1960s, the freedom to practice religion was sharply curtailed in Cuba. After a short conciliatory period, confrontation escalated between Church and State over education reforms, because these explicitly solidified the secular nature of public schools and proscribed religious instruction in them. In addition, the Church was viewed as a potential force for mass opposition to the new government. Both the Catholic and Protestant Churches at times encouraged counterrevolutionary activity, and as a result many churches were closed. Church activity resumed after a national congress on the relationship of Church and State led to a policy revision. The government granted religious believers more freedom to worship and encouraged them to join the Communist party, thus acknowledging the possibiiltity that religious and revolutionary activity could co-exist.[3]

Nationalization of the economy eliminated most sectors of the former economy, including real estate, insurance, law, and banking. The lack of internal investment and a U.S. trade embargo stalled economic development and Cuba became increasingly dependent on aid from the Soviet Union, which agreed to purchase the balance of the U.S. sugar quota left unsold to other nations. As early as 1961, about one half of Cuban exports and some 40% of imports relied on the Soviet market. Cuba's dependency on the Eastern bloc continued until its disintegration and the fall of the Soviet Union in 1991.

Whether for ideological, economic, or creative reasons, most professional architects—about 90% of whom worked in Havana—departed Cuba as a result of revolutionary policies. However, the first romantic phase of the revolution did offer a short-lived climate of creativity for a limited group of building professionals working within, or just outside of, centralized policy. Some were foreign sympathizers of the revolutionary cause, invited to the country by the new Minister of Construction, Osmany Cienfuegos. Others were pro-revolutionary sympathizers living in exile before 1959. Still others were part of an informal group of creative thinkers assembled by Célia Sanchez, a prominent figure in the Cuban avant-garde who sought to explore the Cuban architectural identity in the contemporary context.[4]

One of the most radical minds of the early, romantic phase of the revolution belonged to Ricardo Porro, a Cuban-born architect of Italian descent from Oriente who returned to the island from exile in Venezuela after 1959. Porro, who moved to Paris in 1966, is best-known for overseeing the design of the National Arts School complex in Havana, the only major expressionist work produced in the euphoric honeymoon period of the revolution.

Another individualist, Walter Betancourt, a North American of Cuban descent, came to the island in support of the revolutionary cause in

1961. A strong sense of material, craft, and context infuse Betancourt's buildings, typically made of brick and carefully layered into multi-level sites. A debt to Frank Lloyd Wright is evident both in a series of small parks he designed in Santiago, and in major commissions, including the Forestry Laboratory in the Sierra Maestra Mountains, and the Velasco Cultural Center (completed by Gilberto Seguí Divinó after Betancourt's death in 1978.)

Most notable among the few other architects to make a prominent mark were Fernando Salinas and Antonio Quintana. Salinas had actually studied in the United States, where he

Of Cuban heritage, the North American architect Walter Betancourt settled in Oriente after the revolution. His Forestry Center in Güisa reflects the influence of Frank Lloyd Wright, who offered Betancourt a job at Taliesin in the 1950s.

worked for both Mies Van der Rohe and Philip Johnson. In Cuba, he played an influential role as theorist and educator, emphasizing a humanist approach that was neglected under central planning. His work includes the planned town of Manicaragua in Las Villas province, and participation in the City University José Antonio Echeverría known as CUJAE (1961–64). Both were early experiments in prefabrication that attempted to individualize the built environment within the parameters of set modules. Quintana, who had remained in Cuba after 1959 and was a member of the Célia Sanchez circle, received the bulk of important State commissions outside of schools and housing. His work is characterized by an effort to link buildings to their setting through the use of natural light and ventilation, open spaces, and multiple viewpoints. This approach is especially evident in such varied projects as the Cosmonauts Hotel in Varadero, the

The Parque del Ajedrez *(right) is one of several vest-pocket parks Walter Betancourt designed for downtown Santiago. The architect experimented with brick, layered into different levels that adjust to the city's hilly topography. The 1979 International Convention Center designed by Antonio Quintana in Havana (below) incorporates courtyard-like lobbies, fountains, and red-tile floors. Broad bands of windows and open areas are designed to bring in views of the surrounding mango, banyon, and trumpetwood trees.*

Joaquín Galvan's 1971 design for the restaurant Las Ruinas *in Lenin Park combined prefabricated panels with fragments of an 18th-century sugar mill.*

Havana Conference Center, and the Heredia Theater in Santiago. A similar sense of context is reflected in *Las Ruinas,* designed by Joaquín Galvan. Located in Havana's Lenin Park, this minimalist open-air restaurant nods to the Cuban past by incorporating the stone fragments of a ruined sugar mill on the site.

Although these few individuals managed their own imprint, the move to centralized industrial planning under the Ministry of Construction—charged with all planning, design, and building in Cuba—rapidly eclipsed the independent voice. In particular, the 1963 Conference of the International Union of Architects in Havana addressed the ideological goal of balancing social inequities and focused the State building program on standardized, utilitarian construction. Based on the redistribution of services and work forces and the developmental shift from city to country, the government adopted the concept of comprehensive territorial planning aimed at consolidating scattered rural populations.

The idea was to integrate agriculture and related industries in new "rural towns," conceived as self-contained and self-sustaining communities with health, school, and recreational services linked to a particular work enterprise. For ex-

ample, La Ya Ya, a new town near Santa Clara, offered housing in four five-story apartment blocks for workers in a cooperative dairy operation. Mass-produced housing, schools, farm buildings, factories, and hotels for Cuban workers (many built on artificial lakes created by new dams) were all deemed essential to this master plan for the "urbanization of the countryside" and directly dependent on prefabricated construction. Emphasis on bringing services to rural areas also resulted in training programs for physicians and healthcare workers as well as construction of new health facilities. By the early 1960s, all Cuban citizens were guaranteed free medical and dental care. By 1976, the state building program had produced about 200 new facilities, including general surgical hospitals, as well as those specializing in maternity, pediatrics, and psychiatry. The island-wide network also established hundreds of clinics, spread from city to remote rural village, that serve as the basis of the Cuban primary health-care system.[5]

A centralized construction program for all types of buildings necessitated an internally manufactured technology that could be applied throughout the island on a uniform basis and with a relatively standardized level of training.

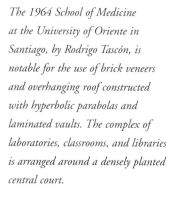

The 1964 School of Medicine at the University of Oriente in Santiago, by Rodrigo Tascón, is notable for the use of brick veneers and overhanging roof constructed with hyperbolic parabolas and laminated vaults. The complex of laboratories, classrooms, and libraries is arranged around a densely planted central court.

Prefabricated concrete forms range from basic functional applications, as in the housing complex at La Ya Ya (left) to the experimental design of the Centro de Investigaciones Científicas in Havana (below), conceived by Joaquín Galvan, Onelia Payrol, Sonia Domínguez, and Carlos Noyola to incorporate two large blocks of offices and laboratories united by a dramatic entrance.

Expansive housing complexes made from prefabricated modules by microbrigade teams in the 1970s, such as the Abel Santamaría District in Santiago, represented a country-wide solution to the housing shortage. Abel Santamaría was a leader in the 1953 attack on the Moncada Garrison.

This included the processing of sugarcane waste for wall partitions and furniture, and experimentation with a variety of concrete prefabrication systems, both open (parts are interchangeable) and closed (parts are not). Among them were the Soviet *Gran Panel* (involving in-place casting) introduced to Cuba in 1963, the Yugoslavian IMS (relying on precast columns and slabs, post-tensioned during installation), and Canadian LH (hollow block).

Efforts to meet an ambitious agricultural production quota in 1970 added considerable impetus to the national prefabrication program. Technology planning centers called "sentry posts" and prefab factories were installed across the island in order to speed construction of roads, dams, dairy centers, and processing plants. By the 1980s, virtually all industrial and farm buildings were built with factory-made columns, beams, panels, slabs, and foundations producing servicable, if featureless, structures of no stylistic note.

PARKS AND MONUMENTS

As public, communal, and highly visible inter-active spaces, parks and monuments play an important symbolic as well as physical role in the revolutionary-period urban landscape. Every city gained a *Plaza de la Revolución;* something new, to be shown off, this was always symbolically located on the outskirts of the city rather than in the old downtown. The administrative heart and soul of Cuba, Havana's *Plaza de la Revolución* is the former *Plaza de la República* remodeled in the 1950s Batista era; the former Ministry of Justice currently houses the Central Committee of the Communist Party, including the offices of Fidel Castro. Like other Cuban plazas, it serves as an important forum for public ceremony; children place flowers here on the anniversary of Che Guevara's death and hundreds of thousands gather for political rallies and Castro's speeches.

New urban spaces born in the early years of the revolutionary government were at once park, monument, *and* plaza. The first important monument completed after the revolution was the Monument Park to Revolutionary Martyrs (1965–67), a national competition won by a team of architects and planners (Emilio Escobar, Mario Coyula, Sonia Domínguez, and Armando Hernández), all of whom had been involved in revolutionary activities during the 1950s. This park/playground located at the site of student rallies near the University of Havana in Vedado is symbolic on every level and served as the model for future projects around

A monument in the Plaza de la Revolución *in Santa Clara honors Che Guevara. Che's capture of the city was a decisive factor in bringing Fidel Castro to power in 1959.*

The 1967 Parque-Monumento del los Mártires Universitarios *in Havana (right and below) combines the function of monument, plaza, and playground, using powerful symbolism to trace the history of political struggle in Cuba. The designers included members and friends of student organizations that fought against Batista; one member of the team was wounded here in 1955.*

the island. It occupies an entire block, and is layered with paths and terraced levels that demand the active participation of the spectator. A series of concrete walls tells the story of student struggles throughout Cuban history; ghostly bas relief images become more nebulous as time progresses and the struggles intensify. The monument's vertical elements suggest positive gains, while the horizontal forms allude to negative resistance to the struggle. The last concrete wedge in the sequence is a broken form that represents Batista's rule; grass grows from the top to signify a new future.

The imagery of Santiago's more recent *Plaza de la Revolución Antonio Maceo* (1991) is equally forceful, but more overt. At the center is a statue of Antonio Maceo, a Santiago-born hero of the independence war, on horseback, offset by a

graduated column of cast-metal machetes. The monument is interesting for its sensitivity to the trapezoidal site, a grassy mound that integrates the low retaining walls and seamlessly incorporates a subterranean building.

On a far more monumental scale, Havana's Lenin Park was an endeavor to create a meaningful green space in an urban setting. Nature itself is the dominant factor in this 1600-acre design overseen by Antonio Quintana, who attempted to identify a natural relationship between the landscape and the new structures introduced into it. Treated almost as sculptures in the larger pastoral context, these include an amphitheater by Hugo D'Acosta and Joaquín Galvan's *Las Ruinas* restaurant. The park also includes a more traditional monument: an overscale bust of Lenin himself.

A dynamic monument incorporating symbolic machetes in the Plaza de la Revolución *of Santiago and inaugurated in 1991 honors Antonio Maceo, a hero of the Independence wars who was born in that city.*

SCHOOLS

The position of education as a fundamental pillar of revolutionary policy was evident in the State's early commitment to building hundreds of schools and eradicating illiteracy (reportedly reduced to 4% by 1962) among children and adults through rural teaching programs. Educating Cubans of all ages was not only a foremost social goal; it was also important to economic development, and a means for building support for the socialist cause through broad-based dissemination of its principles.

All private schools were nationalized. Military barracks of the Batista administration were immediately converted by the addition of desks and blackboards into educational facilities. Further, a program was devised for constructing schools across the island. Among the new facilities were day nurseries and kindergartens, simple rural primary and secondary schools, vocational schools, university complexes, and at least one experimental "school city" (*Ciudad Escolar*) in Oriente. The program produced 17,600 classrooms in the first two years of the revolutionary period alone.

The initial guiding force behind the educational building program was a team of archi-

tects and planners at the *Grupo Nacional de Construcciones Escolares de DESA* (now part of the Ministry of Construction). The DESA concept, which embodied the centralized team approach to design, outlined a standard program for all schools—regardless of size or function. This provided for classrooms and laboratories, dormitories, kitchen and dining rooms, sports facilities, and social areas. To accommodate these needs, the group director, Josefina Rebellón, devised a flexible system of prefabricated concrete modules known as the Girón system. These could be combined in a variety of ways with particular colors and groupings used to identify different spatial functions.

The most successful use of prefabricated concrete modules in school design is widely regarded to be the *Ciudad Universitaria José Antonio Echeverría* (1961–69). Construction of this central technical university known as CUJAE south of Havana involved a lift-slab technology in which the slabs were poured in place and positioned over prefabricated columns with hydraulic lifts; light panels of Siporex form interior additions. The presiding team of designers, made up of Humberto Alonso, Manuel Rubio, José Fernandez, Fernando Salinas, and Josefina

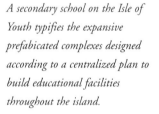

A secondary school on the Isle of Youth typifies the expansive prefabicated complexes designed according to a centralized plan to build educational facilities throughout the island.

Motalván, conceived the school as a group of related buildings (rather than isolated units) of modulated heights and varying levels designed to allow possible later additions. Each facility was connected to another by structural elements—terraced walkways, beamed overhangs, balconies, and loggias—and melded into a whole by means of a series of intimate open and enclosed courts and green spaces.

While CUJAE was underway, designs were also in the works for Ricardo Porro's National Arts School (1962–65), a five-school complex situated on the former golf course of a pre-revolutionary country club in Havana's lush western suburb of Cubanacán, formerly known as Country Club. Headed by Porro, the project was conceived in collaboration with Italian architects Vittorio Garatti and Roberto Gottardi (all three had worked together in Venezuela prior to the revolution). Porro designed the schools of modern dance and plastic arts, Vittorio Garrati created the schools of music and ballet, and Gottardi was responsible for the School of Dramatic Arts. As a whole, the school was intended to celebrate the country's popular roots and make arts education more widely available to Cubans.

The technocratic CUJAE project and the supremely individualistic National Arts School were vastly different, but they did share some underlying constants. Both complexes were team efforts. Both were designed to relate directly to their natural environs and topography. Both comprised village-like groupings, with studios, classrooms, offices, and dining facilities as part of a comprehensive whole. The two projects were also conceived as symbols of evolution, change, and a new open society.

Yet, in distinct contrast to the mass-produced materials and rigid rectilinear forms that put CUJAE squarely in the techno-industrial age, the National Arts School design was organic, steeped in sexual connotations, and rooted in Cuban tradition. Porro's design for the School of Plastic Arts, built of locally made Cuban brick, for example, comprised a series of elliptical, naturally lit spaces protected by curving Catalonian vaults. Snaking through the tropical vegetation, the building was meant to synthesize a kind of female earthiness, the mysticism of the African religious rites infusing Cuban culture, and the sensual appeal he attributed to the Spanish baroque. This extreme-

ly individualistic project fell victim to state criticism of its "hedonistic" design and a shortage of building materials necessary for its completion; some of the buildings for the National Arts School were left unfinished. Many of the buildings now stand in ruins, enveloped by the encroaching tropical vegetation.

Together, the Arts School and CUJAE represent a symbolic fork in the road for Cuba's early revolutionary period: CUJAE was the path taken, and the National Arts School the path not.

The 1970s University complex known as CUJAE, *located south of Havana, reflects an attempt to create an individualistic design using prefabricated units.*

The Havana School of the Arts,
overseen by Ricardo Porro,
incorporates elegant Catalonian
vaults of brick in a deliberate move
away from reinforced concrete. The
evocative buildings were conceived
right after the revolution at a time,
said Porro, "when everything still
seemed possible."

HOUSING

Virtually all revolutionary-period residential construction efforts focused on prefabricated mass public housing projects. These were built on the outskirts of existing cities (such as *La Habana del Este* and Santiago's José Martí district) or as part of the new rural towns dropped into the countryside. The initial State housing effort resulted in about 17,000 new units per year. (Some housing was provided when about 135,000 houses and apartments were confiscated from families that left the island between 1959 and 1975. However, most of these were in the cities and the greatest need was in the country.) But by the mid 1960s, most of the experienced architects, engineers, and builders had left the country. A shortage of materials and skilled design and building professionals, coupled with the focus on health, education, and agro-industrial projects, reduced the annual

housing production to only about 7,000 new units. Meanwhile, the focus on the countryside exacerbated problems in the city. Left to deteriorate, thousands of older houses collapsed (25,000 in 1979 alone), forcing as many families into temporary jerry-built shelters that eventually became permanent.[6]

On the drawing board by April, 1959, the first revolutionary urban housing experiment was *La Habana del Este,* a project of four-to-eleven-story prefabricated concrete apartment blocks planned for 10,000 people in an area east of the Havana harbor Batista had slated for development during his final term. The concept underlying the vast state-sponsored project, devised by a team of architects and engineers including Roberto Carranzana and Mario González, was to provide housing and services (day care, stores, and laundries) in self-sufficient "superblocks" integrated by a variety of public green spaces and

Apartment buildings for La Habana del Este *(left) were conceived shortly after the revolution in an area Fulgencio Batista had set aside for his own development scheme involving a new Presidential Palace. The José Martí district in Santiago (below) includes land for a community garden.*

THE REVOLUTIONARY ERA

pedestrian malls. This idea was partly founded in the post-World War I movement for fixed-rent low- and lower-middle income public housing in Britain and Europe, in which nonprofit and government-subsidy initiatives replaced private speculating. Minimizing the role of the street and automobile traffic, these early projects grouped semidetached or terrace houses around small courts, or consisted of low-rise apartment blocks, articulated by terraces and balconies, set around large planted courtyards and playgrounds, as in the 1927 socialist housing project, Karl Marx Hof, in Vienna.

Built during the first bloom of the revolution, *La Habana del Este* was initially touted as the model for future revolutionary housing schemes, but was later criticized by Cuban planners for its isolating nature and failure to create an "urban sense of life."

Fernando Salinas's design for Manicaragua in Las Villas is generally considered to be more humanizing. This complex incorporated an axial street intended for social interaction and a formal plan of three basic precast molds that played off of concave shapes that provided some measure of stylistic interest.

Fifty miles west of Havana, the new community of *Las Terrazas,* designed by Mario Girona, was a notable exception to the comprehensive apartment-block approach. In 1967, the State designated a 12,500-acre area in the Sierra del Rosario Reserve of the Biosphere near the town of Saroa in Pinar del Río province for reforestation. The reconfigured topography, terraced to permit replanting, accommodated small two- and three-room tile-roof houses, built on stilts and tucked into each level. Foreshadowing the microbrigade teamwork of the 1970s, teams of *campesinos* recruited to work on the forestry project were trained to build the houses they would live in.

After a hiatus in the late 1960s, housing construction accelerated in the next decade, as Cuba was better able to implement systems pro-

Mario Girona's design for Las Terrazas *in the Sierra del Rosario Reserve favored individual houses instead of massive apartment complexes. Workers recruited for the forestry project here were trained in building skills so they could construct their own housing.*

duced by its own prefabrication factories built throughout the island in the preceding years. Impetus also came from microbrigades. These small, localized building teams were introduced in 1970 during a period of modified decentralization, when the state sought new ways to meet a broad range of shortages resulting from the failed effort to meet the ten-million-ton sugar harvest that year.

Microbrigade housing consisted of huge apartment complexes housing 50,000 to 100,000 residents in multifamily apartment blocks (including both four- and five-story walkups as well as elevator towers) serving the population of major cities like Havana and Santiago. The microbrigade effort also produced low-cost one- and two-story buildings for rural villages, sugar-mill centers, and state farms throughout the island.

Each microbrigade consisted of workers temporarily borrowed from their normal jobs at local factories and work centers and assigned to a group of thirty-three members. Once established, the team was taught building skills on the job by professional architects and engineers from the Ministry of Construction. A portion of the apartments in the completed housing complexes was turned over to the work centers that contributed the team members, while the balance went to families being relocated to the new housing centers designed to serve the new rural towns being created. For example, the 1976 complex of *Alamar* in East Havana, designed to combine housing and work centers in the same area, includes three-to-five bedroom apartments, stores, schools, theaters, factories, parks, daycare centers, and recreational facilities contained in prefabricated and hand-built structures. A variety of enterprises, including the Cuban Institute of Oil Research, tobacco centers, the Ministry of Agriculture, and the Merchant Marine all donated microbrigade teams to build this three-and-a-half square-mile project. Sources for materials were diverse: wall partitions were made of processed

The 1976 microbrigade project of Alamar *in East Havana incorporates low-rise apartment buildings, green space, and community services. Intended for 40,000 people, it now houses close to 100,000.*

sugar cane waste, wiring was imported from China, stoves purchased from North Korea, and the plumbing provided by the Soviet Union.

Although it had succeeded in eradicating slum conditions, the Cuban housing effort still fell short by an estimated one million units by the end of the 1970s.[7] To supplement the state projects, 1984 legislation authorized free market sales of land and residential property and

government loans for purchasing the same. Reported abuses led to the restriction of sales again two years later.

The microbrigade effort continued until the collapse of the Eastern Bloc in 1989, and the eventual loss of Soviet subsidies in 1992 cut off the funds necessary to purchase building supplies as well as to run Cuba's own prefabrication plants.

With the shortage of gas and automobiles, families stay home, and television-watching remains a popular pastime in crowded apartment buildings.

CUBA: 400 YEARS OF ARCHITECTURAL HERITAGE

CUBA TODAY

The large-scale projects of the 1960s and 1970s have received mixed reviews. The adjustment from rural life to multifamily living in large urbanized projects was difficult for many, although an effort was made to group families from the same areas together in the new towns. In urban projects like Alamar, some said, houses were built, but the life of the city was missing.

Even the lower, four- and five-story apartment blocks in rural areas have been criticized for imposing an urban pattern where it doesn't belong. Finding himself on the top story of a multifamily complex, a *campesino* accustomed to rural living faced many of the same disadvantages as an urban dweller, only now these drawbacks had become prevalent in the country. Prefabrication systems based on models for northern countries

A small apartment building designed for Old Havana in the 1980s reflects an interest in postmodern design, evident in the ziggurat-shaped roofline and geometric windows.

were invariably ill-suited to a tropical climate and the concrete construction has deteriorated significantly, so the problem of devising systems to address local building needs was never completely solved.

After the loss of Soviet subsidies in 1992, the State declared a "Special Period in Peacetime," during which all Cubans were asked to overcome hardships with creative solutions. Cubans—always resourceful—often make do with clever adaptations from scavenged materials. In its way, the Special Period proved a kind of natural filter. The concept of urban high-rise towers made vulnerable by technical problems was abandoned in favor of smaller projects. A renewed microbrigade program since the onset of the Special Period has begun work on housing developments typically limited to six or eight single- or double-family houses. In addition, a new microbrigade effort has also been designed to renovate existing buildings. The program is intended to provide materials to the residents, who are trained by architects and engineers to work on the houses and apartments they already live in. This plan has been implemented in the Cayo Hueso neighborhood of Havana, where each government ministry has adopted a street and formed a team.

A residence in Santa Clara (right) shows a move in microbrigade housing projects toward single-family houses. The Cayo Hueso neighborhood in Havana (below) has been restored by residents with help from government ministries, which adopted individual streets.

Ingenuity is an inherent part of the Cuban character: Ramiro Heriberto González Rodríguez embedded empty bottles in concrete to build his family house in Congoles (left). The entire town pitched in to help. Guano-thatched roofs in La Tumbita (below) revive the native Arawak tradition of building.

During the early years of the revolutionary period, meeting the immediate needs of the Cuban people placed architectural training at the university level in the rigid framework of centralized planning. It has remained there ever since. However, in the mid-1980s, a period of creative exploration among young Cuban architects coincided with a brief period of relative prosperity. In particular, the 270-room *Hotel Santiago* by José Antonio Choy and two diminutive microbrigade apartment buildings by Eduardo Luis Rodríguez in Old Havana are examples of the few Cuban-designed buildings influenced by the postmodern movement to make it off the drawing board. Rodríguez's projects are notable for their attempt to work within the scale and aesthetic sensibilities of Havana's most important historic district. Their strong, angular profiles and proclivity for postmodernist trademarks (like the four-square window) echo familiar treatments of the style, while such elements as the interior courtyard (criticized by the state-assigned architect as occupying too much space) bring to bear Cuban tradition.

During the Special Period, a complete lack of finances and materials—both domestic and imported—has precluded any major building projects outside of the tourist industry. The 1991 Pan American Village near Cojímar, including a hotel, apartments, sports pavilions, and a stadium built for the Pan American games, is the last planned Cuban town to be constructed. Major building activity is concentrated on new hotels, most notably in Varadero and the Monte Barreto section of Havana, but also in Santa Lucía, Cayo Levisa, Cayo Coco, Marea del Portillo, and Santiago.

The Hotel Santiago *was begun in 1986 during a limited construction boom. It was designed by José Antonio Choy, who explored the use of massive geometric forms and primary colors in a postmodernist design on the outskirts of the city.*

Eduardo Luis Rodríguez's design for the Consultorio y Viviendas del Médico de la Familia, *a small apartment building and clinic, was an effort to fit a new structure into the context of Old Havana. Designed to preserve the scale of the district, the three-story building combines such traditional Cuban features as galleries and an inner courtyard.*

CUBA: 400 YEARS OF ARCHITECTURAL HERITAGE

Miguel Quintero's project for new housing in Van Van and Venceremos, former slum districts in Santiago, focused on small blocks of two-and three-room apartments (left); balconies and changing surface plans bring texture and variety to the facades. The 1950 Acapulco *gas station (below) was redesigned by Herbierto Durerger with postmodernist detailing in 1990.*

The Pan American Village
near Cojímar included a
"main street" of apartments,
shops, and services (right). It
was designed by a team
headed by Roberto Caballero
to house visiting athletes
during the 1991 Pan
American Games. The 1977
sports complex Ateneo
Deportivo Armando
Maestre (below) was the
first building in Santiago to
employ prefabricated
structural units of metal.

In a time of economic strife, this development is not surprising. Immediately following the revolution, Castro had condemned all forms of tourism as imperialist decadence. Existing hotels were confiscated; some were retained for domestic travel while others were turned over to non-travel-related uses. While construction of the first revolutionary-period hotels began in the 1970s, these prefabricated structures were intended for vacationing Cuban workers. The business of foreign tourism began anew in the same decade, when the Cuban State began to trade blocks of empty rooms in winter (the Cuban off-season) to Eastern bloc countries, Spain, and Canada in return for goods such as oil and machinery. In the late 1970s, business picked up more as travel companies formed to serve exiles visiting the island for brief family reunions.

As income from tourism grew, hotel accommodations were improved in the 1980s. Today, tourism is the fastest growing industry in Cuba and second only in income to sugar production. As recently as 1984, Cuba attracted fewer than 200,000 foreign visitors; in ten years that number had tripled—double the average annual figure of the Batista years. A State

tourism development of the late 1980s identified a 300-million-dollar investment in eleven tourism facilities for Monte Barreto. Thirty thousand hotel rooms for Varadero alone are planned for the year 2000; the annual rate of visitors is expected to reach five million by the same date. The majority of the new hotels are joint ventures between Cuba and foreign investors, primarily from Spain, Mexico, France, Germany, Italy, the Netherlands, and Canada. Usually managed by the foreign partner, the new hotels are often recreations of projects that have been designed and built in other resort locations like Cancún, and bear little if any relationship to their settings.

Tourism is directly linked to Cuba's recent acceleration of preservation efforts. Although city centers deteriorated badly when building efforts were redirected to the countryside, neglect also ironically saved them because scarcity has precluded development. Unblemished by new construction, the partially restored historic neighborhoods of such 16th-century cities as Havana, Trinidad, and Santiago now constitute one of Cuba's most important economic resources by attracting tourists.

The Pan American Stadium, by Emilio Castro, originated as part of the 1991 Pan American Games complex, which also comprised gymnasiums, swimming pools, and a tennis center.

The Hotel Moka *by Mario Girona at Las Terrazas (top) makes use of the traditional Cuban gallery and clay roof tiles. The gallery is updated in the Cosmonauts Hotel in Varadero (above); the building, by Antonio Quintana, appears to rest solely on four pillars rising from the sand, but is actually supported by a 1100-ton steel beam that was put in place with hydraulic lifts. The Spanish-managed* Hotel Meliá *in Varadero (right) typifies the vast resort complexes developed under joint ventures in the 1990s.*

Broad-based preservation activity in Cuba is a relatively new phenomenon. Although an article in the Cuban constitution provided for the preservation of monuments and cites as early as 1940, efforts before the 1959 revolution generally did not have broad popular support and were limited to the most famous landmarks, such as the *Plaza de Armas* and *El Morro*. By contrast to sporadic efforts of the post-World War II years, the revolutionary government has shaped a powerful legal mechanism designed to protect individual monuments, entire towns (including the seven original Spanish *villas* colonized between 1512 and 1515), and natural sites.

The national preservation program is administered jointly by the Academy of Sciences and the Council of Patrimony, a component of the Ministry of Culture, itself part of an extensive Council of Ministers. In addition, the cur-

Ongoing conservation projects in historic centers necessitate the revival of traditional crafts; an artisan works in Old Havana (right). Test bands in the decorative cenefa *in Guachinango, a Trinidad* ingenio, *reveal underlayers of earlier painting (below).*

CUBA: 400 YEARS OF ARCHITECTURAL HERITAGE

A craftsman repairs the louvered blinds, or persianas, *in the 17th-century* Colegio de San Ambrosio, *restored as a restaurant and museum called the* Casa de los Arabes *in Old Havana.*

Rehabilitation of the badly deteriorated Malecón will cover fourteen square blocks. More than one half of the fifty-million-dollar budget represents government funding from Spain.

rent 1976 constitution contains two important provisions, Laws One and Two, which respectively define the "national patrimony" (the actual physical legacy of Cuban history, including artworks and buildings) and the "national heritage" (a more abstract concept of cumulative cultural worth). The Havana-based group, CENCREM (*Centro Nacional de Conservacion, Restauración y Museologia*), which inventories and assesses the value of historic sites throughout the country and determines the national preservation strategy, was founded in 1982, the same year UNESCO recognized the international historical and archeological value of Old Havana by declaring it a World Heritage Site. (Trinidad and the *Valle de los Ingenios* were also jointly declared a World Heritage Site six years later.)

CUBA: 400 YEARS OF ARCHITECTURAL HERITAGE

In an approach paralleling a general western trend in preservation philosophy, the Cuban state has moved away from the restoration of isolated monuments and stresses a contextual approach to preserving "living cities" that try to avoid a museum environment and keep the existing population living where it is. Current policy in Old Havana is a prime example. One of the most popular tourist destinations in Cuba, this section of the colonial capital covers the heart of the original walled city founded in 1514. A 214-hectare area (about 528 acres) containing some 4000 buildings in Spanish baroque, neocolonial, and art nouveau styles is currently the subject of an exhaustive computerized study by the Office of the City Historian, which is preparing a detailed master plan for the district to guide restoration and tourism efforts.

Restoration of the 17th-century Casa del Marino, *a small house contained in a cloister of the Convent of Santa Clara de Asís in Havana, was completed in 1996. The building now offers overnight accommodations to visiting scholars.*

The 19th-century interior ironwork and tinted mediopuntos *of the former* Casa de Santiago C. Burnham *in Havana were restored in 1993. The building now serves as the* Casa Simón Bolívar.

To satisfy a mix of needs for both foreign visitors and the Cuban community, structures are ranked into one of four levels according to their historical and physical value. High-level buildings are reserved for museums; the second level for hotels, schools, offices, and restaurants; and the two lowest, which can theoretically tolerate the most intrusion, are designated for housing. However, while housing shortages in the area remain acute, the lack of materials and funds keeps most residences unrehabilitated. The majority of preservation efforts focus on income-producing tourist facilities such as cafes and hotels, which are often housed in 18th-century palaces. Nevertheless, as restoration projects are underway across the island, Cubans now regard the reclamation of historic buildings and neighborhoods as critical to preserving an unbroken line of cultural heritage in the ongoing quest for a Cuban identity.

Restoration plans for the Plaza Vieja *in Havana include the removal of a subterranean parking lot, added in 1952, and renovation of former 18th-century Creole palaces as apartments.*

TIMELINE OF CUBAN HISTORY

C. 1000 B.C.–c.1000 A.D.: Ciboney Indians migrate to central-western Cuba.

C. 800–c.1450: Successive migrations of Arawak Indians (Sub-Taíno and Taíno) largely displace Ciboney.

1469: Ferdinand II of Aragon marries Isabella of Castille.

1479: Ferdinand II succeeds to crown of Aragon.

1492: Official surrender of Muslim power in Spain; Christopher Columbus discovers Cuba.

1494: Treaty of Tordesillas; Spain and Portugal divide New World.

1512: Diego Velázquez de Cuéllar establishes first Cuban settlement of Baracoa; by 1515 seven cities founded.

1515: Santiago de Cuba established as Cuban capital.

1516–56: Reign of Charles I, ruler of the Netherlands and heir to Hapsburg dominions in Austria and southern Germany, in Spain.

1519: San Cristóbal de Habana relocated to north coast of Cuba from original site at Batabanó on south coast; Mexico discovered.

1522–33: Last major Indian uprising.

1523–24: First large-scale shipment of African slaves sent to Cuba to work in mines.

1553: Governor's seat moves from Santiago to Havana.

1556–98: Reign of Philip II in Spain.

1561: System of Spanish fleets established.

1573: New Laws of the Indies codified.

1592: Philip II bestows village of Havana with title of city; *Zanja Real* aqueduct built in Havana.

1598–1621: Reign of Philip III in Spain.

1607: Cuba organized into two governing regions and Havana officially recognized as capital by Royal decree.

1639–50: Construction of first defense system completed in Havana (*Fuerte de Santa Dorotea de Luna de la Chorrera, Fuerte de Cojímar, Torreón de Bacuranao*, and *Torreón de San Lázaro*).

1665: Fortified walls surrounding Havana begun.

1665–1700: Reign of Charles II in Spain.

1697: Peace of Rijswijk ends pirating in Caribbean.

1700: Spain passes to Bourbons; Duc d'Anjou crowned Philip V (1700–46).

1717: First armed insurrection in Cuba against Spanish monopolies (tobacco).

1723: First Cuban printing press established.

1728: University of Havana (*Real y Pontificia Universidad de San Jerónimo de La Habana*) is founded.

1733: All Cuban administrative units put under jurisdiction of Havana.

1746–59: Reign of Ferdinand VI in Spain.

1748: Havana established as a bishopric.

1759–88: Reign of Charles III ("the Reformer's King") in Spain.

1762: England declares war on Spain; Havana and western half of Cuba ceded to England; Havana becomes open port.

1763: Spain receives Cuba back from England under Treaty of Paris, which ends Seven Years' War; Felipe de Fonsdeviela y Ondeano, Marqués de la Torre, becomes new governor of Cuba.

1767: Jesuits expelled from Spain and Spanish America.

1788–1808: Reign of Charles IV in Spain.

1789: French Revolution erupts; Cuba divided into two ecclesiastical jurisdictions (eastern half under Bishop of Santiago de Cuba; western part, with Florida and Louisiana, under new bishopric of Havana); free slave trade is authorized by royal decree.

1791: Haitian Revolution; sugar and coffee planters flee to Cuba, which becomes main sugar producer and slave importer in Caribbean.

1792: *La Sociedad Económica de Amigos del País* chartered.

1793: First public library.

1794: First steam engine imported.

1808: Spanish Crown collapses before Napoleon, who places

his brother Joseph on Spanish throne; Thomas Jefferson attempts to purchase Cuba from Spain.

1809–10: Román de la Luz and Joaquín Infante lead first movement for Cuban independence, including Creoles and free Blacks.

1810–26: Independence wars in mainland Latin American colonies cause migration of Spanish loyalists to Cuba, recognized officially as the "Ever-Faithful Isle."

1811: First Cuban opera company founded.

1814–33: Reign of Ferdinand VII in Spain.

1818: Cuba opens to free international trade.

1819: First steamboat service.

1820: Spain abolishes slave trade (not enforced in Cuba).

1833: Isabella II takes Spanish throne.

1837: First railroad in Latin America inaugurated in Cuba.

1843–44: Slave rebellions erupt on Matanzas sugar plantations.

1847: *Club de La Habana,* center of Creole movement for annexation to the United States, founded.

1848: U.S. President James Polk attempts to purchase Cuba.

1850: Cuban planters lead and finance expeditions against Spanish garrisons.

1853: José Martí (José Julian Martí Pérez), poet, orator, and hero of national independence movement, born.

1853–73: More than 132,000 Chinese coolies shipped to Cuba under eight-year contracts.

1857: Sugar market collapses.

1863: Havana city walls torn down.

1865: Reformist party founded.

1868: Carlos Manuel de Céspedes frees slaves and sets off Ten Years' War of Independence; Isabella II deposed.

1875: Spanish monarchy restored.

1878: Cuba signs armistice with Spain (Treaty of Zanjón) to end Ten Years' War but does not win independence; island organized into six civil provinces: Pinar del Río, Havana, Matanzas, Santa Clara, Puerto Príncipe, and Santiago de Cuba.

1880–86: Slavery abolished.

1892: José Martí initiates plans for general uprising, forming Cuban Revolutionary Party in Tampa, Florida; Cuban plantations yield first one-million-ton sugar harvest.

1895: Second War of Independence begins; José Martí killed.

1898: U.S. enters struggle to support Cuban independence effort; U.S.S. Maine explodes and sinks in Havana harbor precipitating Spanish-American War; sovereignty of Cuba passes to U.S. General Shafter (July 17) under Treaty of Paris and U.S. establishes first formal military occupation and temporary government.

1901: Cuban constitution drafted; U.S. enacts Platt Amendment, securing right to intervene in Cuban affairs; Tomás Estrada Palma elected president; first automobiles in Havana.

1902: Sovereignty passes from U.S. to Cuba and Republic of Cuba established (May 20).

1903: U.S. constructs naval base at Guantánamo.

1904: Cuba holds first elections for national Congress.

1906–09: Liberal factions rebel against Estrada Palma; U.S. military re-occupies Cuba and establishes provisional government.

1908: José Miguel Gomez elected to four-year presidential term.

1912: Mario Menocal elected to four-year presidential term (reelected in 1916).

1917: Cuba declares war on Germany.

1920: Alfredo Zayas elected president; between February and May, 1920, sugar prices peak in the famed "Dance of the Millions," then plunge in December, causing economic crisis.

1924: Gerardo Machado elected president.

1925: Cuban communist party founded in Havana.

1928: Gerardo Machado elected to second, six-year term.

1933: Gerardo Machado exiled to Miami; Carlos Manuel de Céspedes and Ramón Grau San Martín become successive presidents.

1934: Grau government overthrown by Fulgencio Batista and Carlos Mendieta installed as president; U.S. nullifies Platt Amendment.

1935: Mendieta resigns under pressure and replaced by José Barnet.

1936: Miguel Mariano Gómez inaugurated president, ousted by Batista, and replaced by Federico Laredo Brú.

1938: Communist party recognized as legal political body.

1940: Fulgencio Batista elected to four-year presidential term; Commission for Monuments, Buildings, and Historic and Artistic Sites formed for Havana.

1942: Cuba declares war on Italy, Germany, and Japan.

1944: Batista loses reelection bid to Grau San Martín.

1948: Carlos Prío Socarrás elected to four-year presidential term.

1950: First television transmission.

1952: Fulgencio Batista seizes power in coup d'état and imposes seven-year dictatorship; gains support of U.S. for anti-Communist, pro-free enterprise policy.

1953: Fidel Castro and followers attack Moncada Garrison in Santiago de Cuba (July 26) in failed attempt to overthrow Batista government.

1954: Batista elected to second four-year term.

1955: Castro trains guerrilla forces in Mexico; collaborates with Ernesto ("Che") Guevara.

1956: Castro returns to Cuba aboard yacht *Granma*.

1957: Castro leads first successful guerrilla operation in Sierra Maestra mountains; members of Directorio and Auténticos resistance groups attack Presidential Palace; Directorio leader José Echeverría is killed.

1959: Batista flees; government relinquishes power to 26 of July Movement; First Agrarian and Urban Reform Laws.

1960: Racial discrimination officially banned; Cuba and Soviet Union reestablish diplomatic relations; major foreign businesses nationalized; Second Urban Reform Law.

1961: Attempted U.S.-sponsored invasion at Bay of Pigs at Playa Girón fails (April 17); U.S. severs diplomatic relations and imposes trade embargo; Castro declares himself Marxist-Leninist.

1962: Cuban Missile Crisis; North American travel to Cuba forbidden; Cuba expelled from Organization of American States (OAS).

1963: Centralized architectural planning initiated; Second Agrarian Reform Law.

1965: Communist Party of Cuba organized.

1967: Che Guevara killed in Bolivia.

1971: First microbrigades established.

1975: Cuban troops enter Angola; Cuba divided into fifteen provinces (Pinar del Río, Havana, City of Havana, Matanzas, Cienfuegos, Villa Clara, Sancti Spíritus, Ciego de Avila, Camagüey, Las Tunas, Holguín, Granma, Santiago, Guantánamo); First Congress of Communist Party of Cuba convenes.

1976: Constitution promulgated.

1980: Castro opens port of Mariel to Cubans wishing to depart to the U.S.; 125,000 leave for U.S. in Mariel boatlift.

1989: Breakup of Communist Bloc.

1990: State declares "Special Period in Peacetime," inaugurating austerity measures.

1992: Cuba loses Soviet subsidies; U.S. enacts Torricelli Bill prohibiting third-country U.S. subsidiaries from trading with Cuba.

1996: U.S. Congress passes Cuba Democratic and Solidarity Act (Helms-Burton) permitting U.S. citizens and nationals to sue in U.S. courts foreign firms investing in expropriated Cuban property.

NOTES

PART ONE

1. See Llillian Llanes, *Apuntes para una Historia sobre los Constructores Cubanos* (Havana: Editorial Letras Cubanas, 1985), Jorge Rigau, *Puerto Rico 1900* (New York: Rizzoli, 1992) and Eduardo Tejeira-Davis, *Roots of Modern Latin American Architecture* (Heidelberg: Deutscher Akademischer Austauschdienst, 1987) for discussions of architectural education and the influence of contemporary journals.

2. Tejeira-Davis, *Roots of Modern Latin American Architecture.*

3. Llanes, *Apuntes para una Historia sobre los Constructores Cubanos.*

4. Tejeira-Davis, *Roots of Modern Latin American Architecture.*

5. Roberto Segre, *Historia de la Arquitectura y el Urbanismo en America Latina y Cuba* (Havana: Facultad de Arquitectura, 1981).

6. Lohania Aruca, Eliana Cardenas and Roberto Segre, *Historia de la Arquitectura y del Urbanismo III: America Latina y Cuba,* 2nd ed. (Havana: Ediciones ENSPES, 1981).

7. John A. Loomis, "'Architecture or Revolution?' The Cuban Experiment," *Other Americas* (Spring/Summer, 1994).

PART THREE

1. Rigau, *Puerto Rico 1900.*

2. Tejeira-Davis, *Roots of Modern Latin-American Architecture.*

3. For a history of the Colón Cemetery, see Lohania Aruca, "The Cristóbal Colón Cemetery in Havana," *The Journal of Decorative and Propaganda Arts,* vol. 22 (Miami: The Wolfson Foundation of Decorative and Propaganda Arts, 1996).

4. Rigau, *Puerto Rico 1900.*

PART FOUR

1. For an excellent economic analysis of the early Republican era, see Louis Pérez, Jr., *Cuba: Between Reform and Revolution* (New York: Oxford University Press, 1995).

2. Pérez, Jr., *Cuba: Between Reform and Revolution.*

3. Hugh Thomas, *Cuba: The Pursuit of Freedom* (New York: Harper & Row, 1971).

4. Pérez, Jr., *Cuba: Between Reform and Revolution.*

5. Felipe Préstamo, "The Architecture of American Sugar Mills: The United Fruit Company," *The Journal of Decorative and Propaganda Arts,* vol. 22 (Miami: The Wolfson Foundation of Decorative and Propaganda Arts, 1996).

6. Mario Coyula Cowley offers a discussion of this phenomenon in his unpublished article, "La Habana de Enero," August, 1994.

7. For details on Havana master plans see Mario González, *About Schemes, Plans and Master Plans for Havana* (Havana: Grupo para el Desarrollo Integral de la Capital, 1995).

8. Jean-Francois Lejeune, "The City as Landscape: Jean Claude Nicolas Forestier and the Great Urban Works of Havana, 1925–30," *The Journal of Decorative and Propaganda Arts,* vol. 22 (Miami: The Wolfson Foundation of Decorative and Propaganda Arts, 1996).

9. Lejeune, "The City as Landscape."

10. Tejeira-Davis, *Roots of Modern Latin-American Architecture.*

11. Jose Gelabert-Navia, "American Architects in Cuba: 1900–1930," *The Journal of Decorative and Propaganda Arts,* vol. 22 (Miami: The Wolfson Foundation of Decorative and Propaganda Arts, 1996).

12. Tejeira-Davis, *Roots of Modern Latin American Architecture.*

13. Ibid.

14. Carlos Venega Fornias, "Havana Between Two Centuries," *The Journal of Decorative and Propaganda Arts,* vol. 22 (Miami: The Wolfson Foundation of Decorative and Propaganda Arts, 1996).

15. Ibid.

16. Ibid.

PART FIVE

1. For statistics on this period, see Pérez, Jr., *Cuba: Between Reform & Revolution.*

2. Mario Lazo, *Dagger in the Heart: American Policy Failures in Cuba* (New York: Funk and Wagnalls, 1968).

3. Pérez, Jr., *Cuba: Between Reform & Revolution.*

4. John Loomis offers a detailed discussion of revolutionary-period architects in his excellent article "'Architecture or Revolution?' The Cuban Experiment."

5. For statistics on health care, see Pérez, Jr., *Cuba: Between Reform & Revolution.*

6. Ibid.

7. Ibid.

SELECT BIBLIOGRAPHY

BOOKS

Aruca, Lohania, Eliana Cardenas and Roberto Segre. *Historia de la Arquitectura y del Urbanismo III: American Latina y Cuba.* Havana: Ediciones ENSPES, 1981.

Bevan, Bernard. *History of Spanish Architecture.* London: B.T. Batsford, 1938.

Bottineau, Yves. *Living Architecture: Iberian-American Baroque.* New York: Grosset and Dunlap, 1970.

Brusone, Julio le Riverend. *La Habana, Espacio y Vida.* Madrid: Editorial MAPFRE, S.A., 1992.

Bullrich, Francisco. *New Directions in Latin American Architecture.* New York: George Brazilier, 1969.

Chase, Gilbert. *Contemporary Art in Latin America: Painting, Graphic Arts, Sculpture, Architecture. New York: Free Press, 1970.*

Cotarelo, Ramón. *Matanzas en su Arquitectura.* Havana: Editorial Letras Cubanas, 1993.

Cueto, Emilio. *Miahle's Colonial Cuba.* Miami: The Historical Association of Southern Florida, 1994.

Fernández, José Manuel. *La Habana Colonial.* Havana: Grupo para el Desarrollo Integral de la Capital, 1995.

Fernández, Ricardo Nuñez. *Land Planning & Development in Havana City: Two Study Cases.* Havana: Grupo para el Desarrollo Integral de la Capital, 1996.

Foner, Philip. *A History of Cuba and its Relations with the United States,* vols. 1 and 2. New York: International Publishers, 1962–63.

González, Mario. *About Schemes, Plans and Master Plans for Havana.* Havana: Grupo para el Desarrollo Integral de la Capital, 1995.

Hitchcock, Henry-Russell. *Latin American Architecture since 1945.* New York: Museum of Modern Art, 1955.

King, Georgiana Goddard. *Mudejar.* Bryn Mawr, Pennsylvania: Bryn Mawr College, Longmans, Green and Co., 1927.

Kostof, Spiro. *A History of Architecture: Settings and Rituals,* 2nd ed. New York: Oxford University Press, 1995.

Kubler, George. *Art and Architecture in Spain and Portugal and their American Dominions.* Baltimore: Penguin Books, 1959.

Kusnetzoff, Fernando, ed. *America Latina en su Arquitectura.* New York: Holmes & Meier, 1981.

Lazo, Mario. *Dagger in the Heart: American Policy Failures in Cuba.* New York: Funk and Wagnalls, 1968.

Llanes, Llilian. *Apuntes para una Historia sobre los Constructores Cubanos.* Havana: Editorial Letras Cubanas, 1985.

Mack, Gerstle and Thomas Gibson. *Architectural Details of Southern Spain.* New York: W. Helburn, Inc., 1928.

Mendez-Plasencia, Miriam and Margarita Suarez. *Museo de Arte Colonial.* Havana: Editorial Letras Cubanas, 1995.

Pérez, Louis, Jr. *Cuba: Between Reform & Revolution.* New York: Oxford University Press, 1995.

—. *Slaves, Sugar and Colonial Society: Travel Accounts of Cuba, 1801–1899.* Wilmington, Delaware: Scholarly Resources, 1992.

Préstamo, Felipe, ed. *Cuba: Arquitectura y Urbanismo.* Miami: Ediciones Universal, 1995.

Rallo, Joaquín and Roberto Segre. *Introduccion Historica a las Estructuras Territoriales y Urbanas de Cuba 1519-1959.* Havana: ISPJAE, Facultad de Arquitectura, 1978.

Rigau, Jorge. *Puerto Rico 1900: Turn-of-the-Century Architecture in the Hispanic Caribbean, 1890-1930.* New York: Rizzoli, 1992.

Rodríguez, Eduardo Luis and María Elena Martín. *Guia de Arquitectura: La Habana Colonial.* Seville, Havana: Junta de Andalucia, Consejería de Obras Públicas y Transportes; Ciudad de la Habana, Dirección Provincial de Planificación Física y Arquitectura, 1995.

—. *La Habana: Map & Guide to 337 Significant Architectural Monuments in the Cuban Capital and its Surroundings.* Darmstadt, Germany: TRIALOG, 1992.

Segre, Roberto. *Arquitectura y Urbanismo Modernos: Capitalismo y Socialismo.* Havana: Editorial Arte y Literatura, 1988.

—. *Historia de la Arquitectura y el Urbanismo en America Latina y Cuba.* Havana: Facultad de Arquitectura, 1981.

—. *Latin America in its Architecture.* New York: Holmes & Meier, 1981.

—. *La Arquitectura de la Revolucíon Cubana.* Montevideo: Universidad de la Republica, Facultad de Arquitectura, 1968.

Séptimo Congreso de la Unión Internacional de Arquitectos. *Cuba: la Arquitectura en los Países en Vías de Desarrollo* (Havana, 1963).

Seventh Congress of the International Union of Architects. *Cuba: Architecture in Countries in the Process of Development* (Havana, 1962).

Simons, Geoffrey. *Cuba: From Conquistador to Castro.* New York: St. Martin's Press, 1996.

Tarr, Jashina Alexander. *A Collaborative Caribbean Preservation Strategy.* Washington, D.C.: Partners for Livable Places and Caribbean Conservation Strategy, 1982.

Tejeira-Davis, Eduardo. *Roots of Modern Latin American Architecture: the Hispano-Caribbean Region from the Late 19th Century to the Recent Past.* Heidelberg: Deutscher Akademischer Austauschdienst, 1987.

Thomas, Hugh. *Cuba: The Pursuit of Freedom.* New York: Harper & Row, 1971.

Suchlicki, Jaime. *The Historical Dictionary of Cuba.* Metuchen, New Jersey: Scarecrow Press, 1988.

UNAICC. *Arquitectura de Cuba,* vol. xli, no. 375 (Havana, 1992).

Weiss y Sanchez, Joaquin. *La Arquitectura Colonial Cubana.* Havana: Editorial Pueblo y Educación, 1985.

ARTICLES

Acosta, Silvio. "La Arquitectura Moderna." *Colegio de Arquitectos de la Habana,* no. 10, vol. xii (November, 1928).

Aruca, Lohania. "The Cristóbal Colón Cemetery in Havana." *The Journal of Decorative and Propaganda Arts,* no. 22 (Miami: The Wolfson Foundation of Decorative and Propaganda Arts, 1996).

Coyula, Mario. "La Habana de Enero." Unpublished article (Havana, 1994).

—. "La Habana Siempre." Unpublished article (Havana, 1996).

Coyula, Mario and Luis Lápidus. "Historic Preservation in Cuba and Latin America." *Other Americas,* Spring/Summer, 1994.

Fornias, Carlos Venegas. "Havana between Two Centuries." *The Journal of Decorative and Propaganda Arts,* no. 22 (Miami: The Wolfson Foundation of Decorative and Propaganda Arts, 1996).

Gelabert-Navia, José. "American Architects in Cuba: 1900-1930." *The Journal of Decorative and Propaganda Arts,* vol. 22 (Miami: The Wolfson Foundation of Decorative and Propaganda Arts, 1996).

Lejeune, Jean-François. "Jean-Claude Nicolas Forestier: The City as Landscape." *New City,* Fall, no. 1 (1991).

—. "The City as Landscape: Jean Claude Nicolas Forestier and the Great Urban Works of Havana, 1925-1930." *The Journal of Decorative and Propaganda Arts,* no. 22 (Miami: The Wolfson Foundation of Decorative and Propaganda Arts, Inc., 1996).

Loomis, John. " 'Architecture or Revolution?' The Cuban Experiment." *Other Americas,* Spring/Summer, 1994.

—. "Walter Betancourt's Quiet Revolution." *Progressive Architecture,* vol. 76, no. 4 (April, 1995).

Menocal, Étienne-Sulpice. "Hallet and the Espada Cemetery: A Note." *The Journal of Decorative and Propaganda Arts,* no. 22 (Miami: The Wolfson Foundation of Decorative and Propaganda Arts, Inc., 1996).

Peña, Victor Echenagusía. "Guachinango: La Imaginación de un Mundo a traves de sus Muros." *Siga la Marcha,* no. 6 (1995).

Porro, Ricardo and Toshio Nakamura. "Ricardo Porro." *A + U: Architecture and Urbanism,* vol. 94, no. 3 (March, 1994).

Préstamo, Felipe. "The Architecture of the American Sugar Mills: The United Fruit Company." *The Journal of Decorative and Propaganda Arts,* no. 22 (Miami: The Wolfson Foundation of Decorative and Propaganda Arts, 1996).

Rigau, Jorge. "No Longer Islands: Dissemination of Architectural Ideas in the Hispanic Caribbean, 1890-1930." *The Journal of Decorative and Propaganda Arts,* no. 20 (Miami: The Wolfson Foundation of Decorative and Propaganda Arts, 1994).

Rodríguez, Eduardo Luis. "The Architectural Avant-Garde: From Art Deco to Modern Regionalism." *The Journal of Decorative and Propaganda Arts,* no. 22 (Miami: The Wolfson Foundation of Decorative and Propaganda Arts, Inc., 1996).

—. "Our Man in Havana." *Interiors,* (July, 1994).

Segre, Roberto. "Havana Deco: Alquima Urbana de la Primera Modernidad." Unpublished paper.

Taut, Bruno. "Naturaleza y Fines de la Arquitectura." *Colegio de Arquitectos de la Habana,* vol. xii, no. 4 (April, 1929).

INDEX

Gulf of Mexico

FLORIDA KEYS

U.S.A.

Straits of Florida

Varadero

★ Havana

Mariel

Matanzas

Cárdenas

LA HABANA

Isabela
de Sagua

Artemisa

Güira de Melena

Güines

Jovellanos

VILLA CL

San
Cristóbal

Colón

Minas de
Matahambre

Surgidero de
Bataband

Santa
Clara

MATANZAS

PINAR DEL RÍO

Aguada de Pasajeros

Arroyos
de Mantua

Pinar
del Río

CIENFUEGOS

Guana

Cienfuegos

La Fé

Nueva
Gerona

Trin

ISLA
DE LA
JUVENTUD

Caribbean Sea

CAYMAN
ISLANDS

LA HABANA

PINAR DEL RÍO

MATANZAS

LAS VILLAS

ISLA
DE
PINOS

CAMAGÜEY

ORIENTE

PROVINCIAL BOUNDARIES BEFORE 1960